The Ageless Spirit

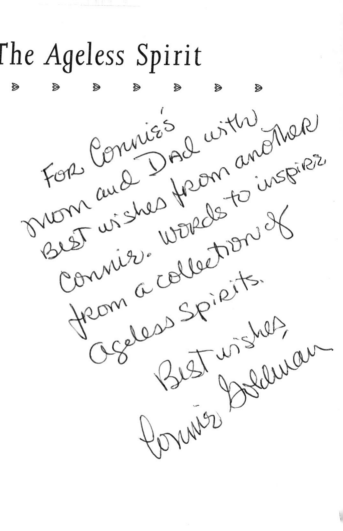

For Connie's Mom and Dad with Best wishes from another Connie. Words to inspire from a collection of Ageless Spirits.

Best wishes,
Connie Goldman

Also by Connie Goldman

The Gifts of Caregiving:
Stories of Hardship, Hope, and Healing

Secrets of Becoming a Late Bloomer:
Extraordinary Ordinary People on the Art of Staying Creative,
Alive, and Aware in Midlife and Beyond
(with Richard Mahler)

Tending the Earth, Mending the Spirit:
The Healing Gifts of Gardening
(with Richard Mahler)

The *Ageless* Spirit

Second Edition

Edited by Connie Goldman

Fairview Press
Minneapolis

Published by Fairview Press, 2450 Riverside Avenue, Minneapolis, MN 55454. Fairview Press is a division of Fairview Health Services, a community-focused health system, affiliated with the University of Minnesota, providing a complete range of services, from the prevention of illness and injury to care for the most complex medical conditions. For a free current catalog of Fairview Press titles, call toll-free 1-800-544-8207, or visit our Web site at www.fairviewpress.org.

First edition © 1992 by Phillip L. Berman and Connie Goldman. Published in the United States by Ballantine Books, a division of Random House, Inc., New York, and simultaneously in Canada by Random House of Canada Limited, Toronto.

Grateful acknowledgment is made to Stanley Kunitz for permission to reprint "The Long Boat" from *Next-to-Last Things: New Poems and Essays.* Copyright © 1983 by Stanley Kunitz. Reprinted by permission of the author.

Library of Congress Cataloging-in-Publication Data
The ageless spirit / edited by Connie Goldman.— 2nd ed.
    p. cm.
  ISBN 1-57749-147-5 (trade pbk. : alk. paper)
  1. Older people—Conduct of life. 2. Celebrities—United States. I. Goldman, Connie.
  BJ1691.B34 2004
  305.26—dc22
                            2004015843

Printed in the United States of America

First printing of second edition: October 2004
08 07 06 05 04   7 6 5 4 3 2 1

Cover design by Laurie Ingram Design (www.laurieingramdesign.com)
Interior design of first edition by Ann Gold

To those in midlife and the years beyond
who choose to look at what they might gain with age,
not what they might lose

Contents

❧ ❧ ❧ ❧ ❧ ❧ ❧ ❧ ❧

Acknowledgments

≫   ≫   ≫   ≫   ≫   ≫   ≫   ≫   ≫

T his book contains the thoughts, experiences, and feelings of fifty-two public figures who were kind enough to take time out of their busy schedules to talk with me. The narratives in this book offer to readers, both young and old, the generous sharing of the wit and wisdom of these special people. I extend to each of them my thanks and gratitude.

My sincere thanks to my support team at Fairview Press, Steve Deger and Joel Meyer, and a special thanks to my wise and patient editor, Lane Stiles.

I've had help and support from friends and family in making this revised edition of The Ageless Spirit possible. I thank them all for their encouragement. Special thanks to Carolyn Mugar, Willie Nelson's colleague at Farm Aid, and to Deanna Wiener, who personally asked Walter Mondale to let me interview him for this book. The people who live with a person writing a book always deserve a thank-you. My partner, Ken Tilsen, has my never-ending appreciation for his wisdom and patience.

Last, but certainly not least, I extend my gratitude to Phillip L. Berman, who co-edited with me the first edition of The Ageless Spirit. Without his encouragement and support, neither version of this book would exist.

Introduction

❧   ❧   ❧   ❧   ❧   ❧   ❧   ❧   ❧

"I challenge you to watch television commercials for a week," says author and aikido black belt holder George Leonard. "You'll see beautiful, incredibly slim young people jumping up and down and throwing frosty cans of diet cola or beer to each other. What does this say to an older person in America? Purely and simply, you're out of the loop. Unless you have the energy and stamina to have one climactic moment after the next, you're doomed, aren't you?"

Americans have an appetite for staying young—no, more than an appetite—an insatiable hunger to remain unwrinkled, thin, and youthful. It seems we want to be accepted for who we were, not who we are, as we push into our sixties, seventies, eighties, and beyond.

But what if the midlife and later years were not something to be feared? What if these years were about creating things, finding purpose, discovering meaning, having fun, and experiencing joy? How different would our later years be if we measured our days not by what we might lose, but what we might gain? What if the midlife years and beyond could be seen as a quest, not a crisis?

We can't ignore the reality that with age often comes illness, frailty, diminished energy, and, in the words of Shakespeare, "the heartaches and the thousand natural shocks that flesh is heir to." But if we nurture a positive, life-affirming attitude, life can have pleasures and rewards at any age.

"I've just had the best year of my life, and I think this every year because I'm continually growing and expanding in every direction," says medical doctor and clown Patch Adams. Peter Yarrow, of Peter, Paul, and Mary, agrees: "I feel every day that I'm in the most exciting period of my life. That probably sounds absurd to younger people, but I have the most vibrant relationships and I'm doing the most meaningful work of my life. I see myself as a work in progress, and I'm continually excited by new possibilities as I continue to grow and gain greater wisdom."

Sometimes, the lives of celebrities may seem very different from our own, but, as you'll discover in the interviews in this book, celebrities face the same challenges that we all face as we age. This book contains conversations with fifty well known personalities. The conversations seldom touch on the topic of fame or indulge in the sort of gossip that often surrounds such celebrities. Rather, they center on the rewards and challenges that come with each new candle we add to our birthday cake.

To understand these rewards and challenges, I asked those I interviewed if they considered growing older a blessing or a curse. Songwriter/performer Willie Nelson answered the question without hesitation: "This is the best time of my life—the fact that I made it this far, that I'm still here, that I'm still healthy. The older I get, the better I feel about things. There's a lot to be picked up if you keep an open mind, an open spirit. I've learned patience, and I've learned to get out of the way, not try to make things happen but let them happen and accept them." Susan Stamberg of National Public Radio responded similarly: "One of the best things for me about getting older is that I've eased up on myself. When I was younger I worked so hard. I was very driven to succeed. Nothing was good enough. Now I've come to a time in my life when I don't feel I have to do that anymore. I'm not sitting on my laurels; I'm using them to step into a more comfortable place."

Actor Ossie Davis believes that one of the main rewards of growing older is the possibility of wisdom: "We never know if we're truly wise. Yet age makes knowledge, tempers knowledge with experience, and out of that comes the possibility of wisdom." He adds, "Age is that point of elevation from which it is easier to see who you are and what it is you want to do, and from which you find yourself closer to the very center of the universe."

Time—its brevity, its preciousness—was a recurring theme in nearly every conversation. "What the years do is rush the passer," said author and pioneer radio dramatist Norman Corwin. "I'm like a quarterback on the run, trying to get rid of the ball before I'm taken down." While there are many disadvantages to feeling like a quarterback on the run, there is also one enormous advantage: you seldom take time for granted. Indeed, one of the greatest blessings of maturity is that time is no longer a commodity to be squandered thoughtlessly on vain and empty pursuits. As time diminishes, its preciousness increases. Historian Arthur Schlesinger, Jr., put it bluntly: "Every once in a while when I go to a boring meeting or dinner I wonder what in the hell I'm doing wasting time. In your seventies, time becomes the most precious of commodities. The thing I resent most is wasting it. Up until the age of seventy, time seems infinite, but time is now finite."

How to make the best use of time presents us all with a vexing conundrum. On the one hand we have strong needs to devote ourselves to activities that are productive and meaningful. On the other hand, after navigating several decades in the world of work and keeping ourselves continually busy, we come to recognize the importance of savoring life's simple pleasures in a state of enlightened equanimity.

The late writer May Sarton spoke of her equanimity, her ability to maintain evenness under the stress of suffering a stroke: "When you're sick, everything is taken from you at once. Yet, in a way, the great advantage of going through something awful is that the ordinary things become so precious. The fact that I can garden is just heaven, and I can enjoy life again." For author Eve Merriam, as well, "a love for the ordinary, not for the extraordinary, is what is most important as one ages. There are always trips to Bali or Yokohama or Paris, but to get joy out of dailyness, that's what struck me when I hit my sixties. I thought, Good heavens, I'm getting so much pleasure out of my breakfast. I didn't know grapefruit juice could taste so good. This is really amazing. It's as though some kind of slight film over the world has been stripped away and there is now a clarity that one didn't have before."

Appreciating the simple things in life often involves a slowing down from the busy pace of earlier years. Charles Schulz, the creator of "Peanuts" put it this way: "Just to hang around is all right, just to sit in a chair and stare into space. It's almost something that has to be learned. I don't feel that I have to be reading something or writing something. I'm great for doing nothing."

But as one ages, there's also time to be busy and productive. Some tackle a new vocation or job; others explore a hobby or develop a unique skill. For others, like photographer Richard Avedon, it's work: "The one thing I believe in is work. If you're lucky enough to have something you want to do, you do it everyday of your life. Work, when I'm done, I have work—that's the bottom line for me."

Performer Kitty Carlisle Hart believes in keeping active, busy, and interested: "You have to find something that really interests you and pursue it ferociously. It doesn't have to be work that pays. I tell people they must never stop, never say that you're too old for this or that. You'll see, we can all do more than we think we can."

Whether we're busy doing something or relaxing and doing nothing, television personality Art Linkletter reminds us that we need to maintain a sense of levity to give life balance: "Humor is the lubricant you need to get through life, and it is particularly important as you age." On the subject of humor and laughter, actor Hume Cronyn quipped: "I don't want to end up with a smooth face. The lines, the wrinkles, let them get deeper, particularly the laugh lines. That's not only what gives life its savor, but it's the thing that charges our batteries."

Yet, it isn't always easy to laugh when life presents us with an unexpected crisis or challenge. That's why courage is also an important ingredient in a healthy recipe for aging. "You have to become much more flexible," declared writer, educator, and family counselor Eda LeShan. " You have to be willing to change, you have to face painful crisis, and courage is absolutely the most essential part of it. Courage implies a lack of denial, that you really are willing to face issues, whatever they are, and that you grow from them—that there's nothing that happens to you as long as you're alive that you don't learn from."

With characteristic optimism Linkletter told me, "I like to think that every day some experience or some new acquaintance or some new challenge is going to change my life. There's always one hill higher with a better view, something waiting to be learned I never knew. So till my days are over my prayer is, 'Never fill my cup, let me go on growing up.'" Former television personality Hugh Downs shared a different but equally optimistic metaphor for aging: "I liken aging to a piece of fruit. You can go from green to rotten without ever ripening, and that's tragic. It's important to mature, to ripen. I suppose that's what I hope for—that I continue to ripen until it's my time to go."

The people you'll meet on the pages of The Ageless Spirit will tell you a great deal about themselves. They'll share their personal stories, experiences, and wisdom. Yet they'll leave you thinking less about who they are and more about who you are and how you can get in touch with your ageless spirit. Many years ago I ran across a quote in *The Measure of My Days*, a book written by Florida Scott Maxwell, that I've shared with many. Maxwell challenges each of us to seek our own ageless spirit:

> A long life makes me feel nearer truth, yet it won't go into words, so how can I convey it?... I want to tell people approaching and perhaps fearing age that it is a time of discovery. If they say—"Of what?" I can only answer, "We must each find out for ourselves, otherwise it won't be discovery." I want to say, "If at the end of your life you have only yourself, it is much. Look, you will find."

The Ageless Spirit

Willie Nelson

➣   ➣   ➣   ➣   ➣   ➣   ➣   ➣   ➣

Even if you're not familiar with Willie Nelson's gospel-flavored, jazz-inflected, country music style, you'd probably recognize a photo of this songwriter-singer-performer, with his cowboy-hippie garb, long red hair, headband, scraggly beard, gently smiling face, and sparkling eyes couched in deep wrinkles. Those who know the living legend well say there's nothing false about him. He's as honest and true as his music. Nelson is powerfully centered in his artistry. Even when he became a star, he never played it safe musically. His style constantly changed as he borrowed from traditional pop, Western swing, jazz, traditional country, cowboy songs, honky tonk, rock and roll, folk, and the blues, creating a distinctive hybrid.

A performer in his seventies might be expected to slow down a little, but not Willie Nelson. He celebrated a recent birthday by releasing a two-CD collection of greatest hits, The Essential Willie Nelson. And he's showing no indication that he intends to stop performing anytime soon. There's always a sold-out show scheduled in the next town, and the bus that currently serves as his home on the road will be leaving soon after this evening's concert in the Wisconsin Dells ends. Before the show started, I had some time to visit with Willie Nelson.

Song writing is a natural thing for me. I think of it as a gift. I was born with this ability. I knew from the beginning that music was where I was going. It was only a matter of when do I get there. Along the way I've learned a little musicianship and singing. I've learned enough playing to accompany myself. I know a lot of singers and many musicians who are far better than I am. What's important to me is, when I perform people feel like I'm talking directly to them. If I can communicate through music, if they can hear what I'm saying, if they believe I'm talking or singing directly to them, that's what I try to do. I think someday I might give up going on the road all the time. But there are worse ways to go out of this life than on stage.

This is the best time of my life—just that I made it this far, I'm still here, and I'm still healthy. The older I get, the better I feel about things. The experience of living has certainly taught me something. I believe you have to keep coming back into this world, that we keep coming back until we get it right. Some of us come through here a few times and never pick up anything. But eventually we can get life right. It's the only thing that really makes sense to me.

There's a lot to be picked up if you keep an open mind, an open spirit. There's wisdom out there. What have I learned? I've learned patience. And I've learned to get out of the way, not try to make things happen but to let them happen and accept them. When you're young you try to control everything. That's where having experience comes in. You find things that work and things that don't work. It's simple: you keep what works and drop what doesn't. You have to trust your instincts. The first thought you have about the right thing for you to do at that moment is probably the right choice. So often we think, "It just couldn't be that simple," and you start to think of other ways to do things, and by then it's too late. Over the years I've learned to just go with my instincts and trust them.

My grandmother raised me and my sister. She was very practical, very religious, went to church regularly and made sure that we went to Sunday school. She was our teacher. She taught us right from wrong, taught us to be independent, and encouraged us both in our music. I don't go to church now because I move around a lot. Each Sunday I'm on tour in a different place. I feel that we all travel around in our own churches. There's something in each of us that remains ageless, remains the same. It's like the glue that keeps us together. You have to follow your instincts and listen to those still, small voices that seem to always tell you right. But you have to be still and listen. One of the best lines in the Bible is "Be still and know that I AM." You've got to get still before you're able to become aware.

I believe in everything and everybody. There's no reason to narrow that down. I have a wonderful family, both relatives and extended family, and lot of fans out there that I think of as my friends. They're part of my family too. They may not be blood-related, but they're definitely family. My ageless spirit is very much connected with your ageless spirit and every other living entity. Once you realize that, life becomes very simple. We're all connected.

Eddie Albert

⤜　⤜　⤜　⤜　⤜　⤜　⤜　⤜　⤜

National Film Critics Award recipient Eddie Albert is perhaps best known for his portrayal of a city man gone country in the long-running television series "Green Acres." Yet he has had a long and acclaimed career in film, including major roles in Oklahoma, The Longest Day, The Heartbreak Kid, Roman Holiday, *and* The Sun Also Rises.

Apart from his career in acting, Eddie Albert is one of America's most distinguished and respected environmental activists. He has conducted lecture tours throughout the country on ecology, participated in The World Hunger Con-

ference, served as a trustee of the National Parks and Recrea-
tion Association, and is chairman of the Eddie Albert World
Trees Foundation. He is eighty-three years old and makes his
home in Southern California.

One of the things that I find so troubling about
growing old in America is that we don't fully
appreciate the value of experience. And who is more
experienced in living than the elderly? As a general rule,
people are not very intelligent. Most of us really don't
know anything about anything if you want to get right
down to it. But we all learn some things through experience. Sometimes we blow it, but we learn through the
experience. Today most of that experience goes down
the drain and out the sewer because we've got early
retirement. Just about the time a man grows up enough
to really lock horns with this fantastic civilization we tell
him to go to sleep.

In a book that Garson Kanin wrote, he recounted a
wonderful story about the great power blackout in one
of our large cities. Apparently the experts spent a couple
of days trying to figure out what went wrong, but
nobody seemed to know. The young engineers were
stumped. Finally they stumbled onto this old guy—he
was about seventy-five or eighty—who had been in the
electrical department years before. He came over to the
power plant and walked around for a while, looking at
this and that lever, and then he said, "Could I have a
hammer, a small hammer?" They gave him a small

hammer and he walked over and tapped on a little connection circuit and the lights went on. And they said that's wonderful, how much do we owe you? He said it would cost them a thousand and one dollars. "What is this? For heaven's sake, you just hit a circuit with a hammer!" He says, "That's one dollar. The thousand dollars is knowing where to tap." And that's experience.

I remember preboarding a plane once when the pilot came back and said hello to me. He was a marvelous-looking man and he sat down alongside of me and said, "I'm very glad to have you on my flight because this is my last flight." I said, "What do you mean?" He said, "I have to retire." I said, "Well, you don't look to me like you're all that old." I think he was fifty-five or sixty—something like that—but he was young and vigorous and he'd flown thousands of miles. He knew how to run that airplane. I said, "What are you going to do?" He says, "Well, I thought I might get a sewing machine and make dresses for my grandchild." And I looked at this poor man and I thought of the poor passengers. He'll be replaced by somebody forty or thirty-five who has not gone through the hell of trying to make a decision about how to land in a storm or in the dark with gale-force winds and things of that sort. The injustice and stupidity of throwing that experience down the drain, out into the sewer, just enraged me. One of the reasons they do it is that it's cheaper for the company. Lower salaries for the newcomers, and more profits for the company, but at the expense and safety of us travelers.

Another reason is the ancient delusion that aging means incompetence. That's probably true of basketball players, and men throwing railroads across the West in the nineteenth century, but today our complicated society requires experienced judgment calls, and that experience only comes with years on the firing line. No other way.

I was recently in Florida at one of those retirement places, talking to some of the men—a couple of admirals and a few CEOs, wonderful guys. And I said, "What do you do?" They said, "Well, we gather about nine o'clock in the morning, bring down the garbage, and then do what we want. Ralph will go off and play some golf and Bill will play cards and. . . ." The list was run off with no enthusiasm at all. Is it any wonder that most men die or are divorced three years after retirement? Or that the odds for suicide multiply twelve times on the day after retirement? They bore themselves to death. These were great men who had great accomplishments and have within themselves the ability to do it again. Now they just sit there.

There is a shortsightedness and selfishness out there, and I find it deeply troubling. Not only do we not value experience, we take a shortsighted approach to almost all of our major national policy decisions. Only recently, for example, I was listening to Henry Kissinger talking about a discussion he'd had with Mao in China on revolutions. He asked Mao what was his estimate of the effect on our present society of the French Revolution of 200 years ago. And Mao thought a minute and said, "It's too early to tell." And this is very, very true. Two hundred years is not a long time. The wars of today will still be echoing 500 years from now. Experienced, thoughtful people already know this. They know that we are very incorrectly rushing around wanting a dividend every three months. And if we don't get some sort of an answer in three months, heads roll or we go crazy.

I remember a visit I took to Japan, where we stopped and looked at a carpentry shop, in Kyoto. In the shop there was a young man and an old man, about ninety-five. They were making wooden boxes to house sacred statues. I asked the old man, "What are you doing?" He told me that he was binding the wood together for seasoning. I asked, "How long do you season this wood?" He answered, "Thirty-five years." And I looked at the old man and he saw me looking at him and he caught on. He said, "No, no, it's not for me, it's for my son." What a different sense of time! What a larger and more generous sense of responsibility! Today, if we don't get some dividend out of it each day, it's considered stupid.

This shortsighted way of looking at things is the reason our environment is such a mess, and the situation is getting ever more desperate day by day. In my work to preserve the earth I encounter this shortsighted mentality almost constantly. I'm working on the drought (in California) right now, and while I'm working on it I tell myself, "Eddie, you've got to look ahead—twenty years at the *minimum*—don't be impatient and scream." You see, I know now that the human race is not going to move that fast, so there's no point in getting excited or calling anybody a villain. For example, I just finished a letter to the governor of California, pointing out that the cutting of trees has a lot to do with the lack of rainfall; that the tree-rain cycle must not be broken. When the public goes into an area and starts cutting the trees, that's the beginning of the end. California has 40,000 new acres of desert every year. At that rate it won't take long to wipe out California. I was suggesting that he put together the youth corps again so that we could plant billions and billions of trees, which will recycle the rain and lessen the drought. But, here again, that's twenty years before the trees mature. There's no point in my getting excited about wanting to see the finish; I won't be here. On the other hand, what is the point in living if you don't do your best to leave the planet a little better for your having lived here?

I happen to be kind of lucky because I'm healthy and I want very much to do positive things with my life. My job now for the next twenty or twenty-five years is to work on the environment. I've got to use my experience to get out and do what I can to knock off this pillage of our natural environment. The way I see it, I've been given a marvelous public image, I've had an income as an actor, and I've enjoyed every bit of it. But I also love nature. My life isn't over yet, so why not have a crack at preserving it? If there's any machinery in the stars, this is what it is for me. Like Joseph Campbell said, "Go for the bliss." The bliss is what you inherit from your past without realizing it. Now, I like nature and I don't like business, so if I'm going to really do anything of any value before I cut out, I have to make a difference *today*.

I don't know what happens in the end, but that's really not my business. California may be in the middle of the Pacific in the next five years, but it's not my affair. I'm in a much better position because I have no hopes, no goals for myself, really, except a satisfaction of doing. If I look at my log at the end of the week and can say, "Hey, you did a good thing there," that's enough. So I can't get pissed off the way I used to.

I'm not altogether sure that I know a whole lot of things, but what I do know is that to lose contact with nature is like throwing gold in the sea and losing it. To have, for example, my lovely garden here every day and not get out in it is a crime. You know, I often come out here in the middle of the night to talk to these lovely plants and flowers. That really gives some people a charge. I remember once the Canadian Broadcasting Corporation came down here to follow me around for two or three days. At the end of the third day the producer finally got up enough nerve to say, "Mr. Albert, I understand you talk to trees." And he was kind of embarrassed because he was urged by higher-ups to "see if you can get him to talk to a tree, get it on film." So I said, "Yeah, I do that." And he said, "Would you do it for the camera?" "Yes." So I did, and I said to the olive tree, "I just want you to know that we really appreciate you here. You make a marvelous contribution to this garden. I remember when my kids used to climb up in you. And I remember the time I made a mistake in fertilization and you got sick and how difficult it was to bring you around. Now I see you've stabilized, but we've lost a lot and I must apologize. I just want you to know that we love you and hope we'll all be together for a long time."

We're part, each of us, of this immense and beautiful planet. And I believe strongly in what Albert Schweitzer called "reverence for life." The German word he used is far more complex than the English. It includes both awe and love. A Jesuit priest in France hit the nail on the head when he said, "Someday, after man has tamed all these energies—the tides, the winds and gravity, and so forth—he will turn his mind toward the power of the energy of love. And for the second time in man's history he will have discovered fire."

Steve Allen

> ⟫ ⟫ ⟫ ⟫ ⟫ ⟫ ⟫ ⟫ ⟫

Television's seventy-year-old Renaissance man is one of the labels used to describe the multitalented comedian and author Steve Allen. At one moment he can be blurting out a hilarious off-the-cuff one-liner; at another, decrying the plight of the downtrodden. His lucid and open mind enables him to move easily from the most complex subjects to zany comedy. He works his brain like a mine on a twenty-four-hour-a-day digging schedule; he finds ideas both when awake and asleep. Always ready to extract them, he has small tape recorders everywhere—in his pockets, by his bed, in his car. This system supplies the raw material for Steve Allen's numerous activities.

I n my capacity as an entertainer, I get a certain kind of respect just for having been around for a long time that I didn't get twenty or thirty years ago. I had no complaints twenty or thirty years ago—both audiences and my peers treated me kindly—but you can just sense there's something different now. I guess it's in the introductory applause when you're brought on stage at some function. That's certainly a plus. Another plus is that as the years pass, I'm better at everything in show business or in the arts than I was ten, twenty, thirty, forty years ago—wherever you want to put the dipstick back in, I'm better now than I was then. My wit comes faster on stage, I play the piano much better, my songwriting ability has improved, I'm writing books faster, and I cannot think of any exceptions to that.

A skeptic might say, "How do you know you are better now than you were years ago?" I answer: I'm writing more jokes per day, I'm much faster in nightclubs or in concert halls, and when suddenly the teleprompter falls down during formal proceedings I can do twelve minutes without its assistance. I'm just better at that. You can tell whether you're better or whether you're losing your powers. So it is therefore demonstrable and measurable.

To refer to someone else, George Burns is now, I think, 412 years old, and he's not interested in retiring.

He's as good as ever. Bob Hope is, I think, only 206, but he's not interested in retiring. And artists, in fact, of any sort—the good and the bad and the medium—have never retired. Did Leonardo da Vinci ever retire? Did Shakespeare retire? No, it would be stupid. If you can still write a poem when you're 100 years old, and if it's a good poem, what's retirement got to do with anything in your life? Nothing.

Retirement, nevertheless, is an absolute necessity for most people. There are certain things eventually you're pretty poor at simply because you're eighty-four years old. If you can't walk across the damn room, what good are you down at the plant? No good at all. That's why you don't see any eighty-six-year-old men in factories (unless they own them). So it's absolutely necessary that we have a policy about retirement and an age at which, in certain contexts, you must retire that make sense.

I think most people who retire are relieved anyway. Most of the world's jobs are boring, coming under the heading of, "Oh, God, if it weren't for the money, why would I do this for a living?" You have to put up with rude customers, and the shoddy merchandise they give you to sell, and all kinds of terrible things. It's a relief to get away from the business world, to finally do all the bridge playing you always wanted, and all the fishing, and all the seeing of foreign ports—whatever's your thrill.

I can't emphasize enough the importance of exercise. It tends to bounce off our heads most of the time because it is such common advice; it bounced off mine for a long while. You would never argue, "Aw, forget it, nobody needs exercise,'' but somehow it doesn't become clear until you're past fifty. My wife, Jane, and I are working harder and harder at taking care of ourselves. The benefits are enormous. When I can get into my pool for about a half-hour vigorous workout I'm better at everything else for the rest of that day. I can dictate seven and a half more letters, I'm faster and funnier with the witty part of my brain, and if I have to go out that night I feel energetic instead of half asleep at the restaurant. It's just common sense to get exercise, unless you're in a hurry to pass the scene.

We all have to acknowledge all eventualities and realities, and one of those is death. We're all going to die, folks, and some of us are going to be lucky enough to die in our sleep and some of us are going to be unlucky enough to get run over by a tank. But, generally, it only takes about twelve seconds to die; you don't have to give a whole weekend to it. Besides, some people are reporting that it isn't so bad on the other side. You hear these stories: ''You were dead for forty-seven seconds.'' ''Well, it's nice to be here anyway.''

Even such simple words as ''death'' are difficult to define. You can obviously look at a hole in the ground and say, ''This guy's been dead for 300 years,'' but it's not that easy to pick out ''the moment of death.'' Your fingernails haven't died yet, your hair hasn't died yet. Many parts of your body are still pumping away; they haven't gotten the message, ''Hey, guys, lay off. We died up here, you know; we don't need you anymore down there.''

I suppose I take a rather humorous approach toward

death, but why not? Humor is very important, not only to those of us who make a living at it, but because it has to do with the attitude that you carry into your daily experiences. You cannot smile your way through everything. If somebody's rude to you, you feel emotionally abused, and you're unhappy for the forty-nine seconds of that experience. But it need not ruin the rest of your day, and it certainly need not ruin your eventual relationship with others. Humor is not just a little frosting on the cake. It is vital, it is necessary, it is uniquely human. We sometimes laugh at what monkeys do, but one monkey never looks at another and says, "Boy, he's funny; he should make a living at that." Only humans are consciously funny, so it is either a gift of the Creator or an accident that fell off the tree of evolution. In either event, we should be damn grateful for it. I am and I think many people are.

If the average reader studies what we've talked about here, he might come away with the realization that "hey, I'm fifty-two now, and when I get to be seventy-two I'm not going to be falling apart the way I thought I was." We carry with us the baggage of centuries of interpretation of what such words as "old" or "age" mean. I still haven't adjusted—and I'm a reasonably intelligent person—because I still carry the image that I got when I was twelve years old. In my childhood, a sixty-year-old woman might as well wrap it up and go to the old folks home; forget it, forget everything, you're too old, you sit in a rocking chair and nod a lot and sleep a lot. Today sixty-year-old women are some of the sexiest-looking women I know. The word "grandmother" used to mean a little old lady with gray hair and heavy glasses and asthma or something. Now there are grandmothers on tennis teams or running for Congress.

John Cage

≥   ≥   ≥   ≥   ≥   ≥   ≥   ≥   ≥

At age seventy-nine John Cage radiates a childlike charm and gentle wit. His life is a busy and active one that includes travel, friends, avocations, diversions, and, of course, his continuing work as a composer. His home and studio are in a large loft in New York City that he shares with the choreographer Merce Cunningham. It houses an indoor garden and hundreds of exotic plants.

As a force in contemporary music, John Cage has monumental stature, although often his compositions and performances have been considered eccentric and monotonous. It's

29

been said he has had a greater impact on world music than any other American composer in the twentieth century. His past works have incorporated such sounds as audio frequency oscillators, buzzers, gongs, sirens, whistles, and silence. Composer Aaron Copland observed that Cage isn't interested in creating great eternal masterpieces but in amusing himself on the highest level with new notions concerning music. John Cage would agree.

My father was an inventor, so I grew up in an atmosphere that stressed the necessity of having new ideas, of making discoveries. From the beginning I knew that the only thing I would be able to do that would be useful to society as a whole would be to make some kind of discovery. My father was still making new inventions in the field of electrical engineering well into late life, so I just put my mind to figuring out where I could make my own creative contributions. I decided upon music, and that's how the whole thing started. I like to think that I'm still making new discoveries every day. I remember a lady in Chicago saying to me, "Oh, when you get older you'll mellow." And the suggestion was that I would get soft and that I would become content more easily and that I wouldn't be looking for something so irritatingly new. But I don't think that's happened.

I am now having one of the most productive years of my life. Looking back, I see that there were certain years when I was more active than others. I was very active in

1952. The number of pieces I wrote that year is quite astonishing, even in retrospect. But this year things are happening nearly as fluently. A string quartet, a piece for organ, eight pieces for oboe, a piece for percussion . . . I just finished nine songs, and that's simply the amount of work up to August.

As I get older I get more concerned about being healthy. I used to think that the mind and spirit, so to speak, were superior to the body. But then the time came when I was on tour with the Merce Cunningham dance company and we were in Venezuela. There I experienced tremendous back pain. I'd always had trouble with my back, but this time it hurt so much that it was painful to do anything. I barely managed to stand up and bow at the end of each performance, it was that bad. Finally, I was helped by a doctor there who gave me a drug to take away the pain. Then he insisted I do certain exercises and continue doing those exercises for the rest of my life. Before, I had never done any, but now I do them every day. What has happened is that I now see that the body is part and parcel of the whole being. There isn't a split between the mind and the body; they both belong together. When I was younger, I mistreated the body because I thought the mind was what I was really dealing with. But as I get older I see that I'm dealing quite straightforwardly with the body and that I must keep it in good working order as long as I can.

As I get older my interests multiply rather than lessen in number. I'm interested in indoor gardening and I'm interested in macrobiotic cooking. My latest interest is the collection of rocks. Now in all my travels I collect either small rocks or, if I have the facility, big ones. I'm not only interested in collecting them to have them in my garden, but I've turned them into the makings of etchings and of drawings and now even into the composition of music, so that my songs are simply made by drawing parts of the rocks.

I think that growing old in a happy way derives from self-employment. If you are self-employed, you will see each day as useful, no matter how old you are. Most people accept jobs that are not interesting in order to make money. In other words, they think that money is important and life is not. What we need to do is to be willing to die for what gives us life. I knew that I loved music and I was willing to die for it, so I didn't approach music as something that would make me money. If I needed money, I would then take a job that would make money, such as washing dishes or distributing fliers or something like that. I wasn't well-to-do until after I was fifty.

For people who were employed all their lives at a job they did for money, retirement is actually a good thing, but they will have to adjust to the self-employment mentality. Better yet, prepare for it *before* you retire. Everyone who went to school learned how to read and write, therefore I have the idea that everyone could work at being a poet. Now, that would be a good job in retirement. You could spend your life writing poetry, and you could begin while you were employed as a secretary or as a computer programmer. You could put aside a little time each day in which you employed yourself to be a poet. Then when you lost your job or were retired, you would know that you could go on writing poetry. And if you didn't like to write poetry or didn't like to write music, you could make a drawing. My drawings are made by drawing around the stones I collect. I don't have to know how to draw. The rock teaches me where to put the pencil.

If you go to sleep, you wake up with energy and you either use that energy yourself in terms of self-employment or use the energy in relation to someone who tells you what to do. If someone is telling you what to do, then I'm advising you to supplement that with telling yourself something to do, so that when they stop telling you something to do you will be able to go on telling yourself what to do.

Unfortunately, too many people think that creativity is something mysterious that only belongs to certain people, whereas everyone has access to it. I had a walk once with Mark Tobey, a great artist. (This was in Seattle.) We walked very slowly because Mark Tobey was constantly seeing something that he wanted to point out. And it wasn't something like a mountain; it was more like cracks in the pavement or something on the wall of a house where something had fallen off. His eye was absolutely open, constantly, to the world around him. And I think that walk not only helped my seeing but also my hearing, so that now I listen all the time to the sounds of the environment of where I am. This year—in contrast to previous years of my life—I'm beginning to hear the constant sounds, like the sound of the humidifier, that I used to ignore in order to hear the more changing sounds of traffic. Most people would ignore traffic in order to hear a little music. But now I'm beginning to be interested in the humidifier and the refrigerator and any other thing when it has a constant kind of sound, which for most people are irritating sounds. Those sounds are beginning to define space for me so that through them I know the nature of the space I'm living in. And it's giving me a great deal of pleasure because those were the sounds that I didn't really accept, that I tried to ignore. Now, more and more, I don't hear anything without enjoying hearing it, including those constant utilitarian sounds. If you can enjoy the worst things, then the rest is easy.

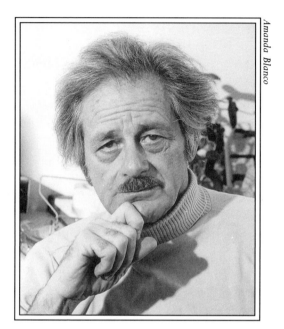

Norman Corwin

⧽ ⧽ ⧽ ⧽ ⧽ ⧽ ⧽ ⧽ ⧽

Writer, director, and pioneer radio-drama producer Norman Corwin began his career in radio in the 1940s as the chief of special projects for the United Nations radio network. Since that time he has produced scores of highly acclaimed books, stage plays, screenplays, and teleplays. The recipient of numerous awards and honorary degrees, he has served as a visiting professor at the University of Southern California since 1981. He is eighty-one years old.

M y father died in 1987 at the age of 110, and he kept his marbles all the way. He had very little wrong with his perceptive powers except that he suffered from short-term memory loss. But he was shrewd enough and smart enough to realize that, so he kept all his comments down to an executive minimum. But I don't seem to have the same genetic powers that my father did because I've already had a cardiac episode. That happened at seventy. In fairness to myself, though, I've lived a much more stressful life than my father. For one thing, he was never a liberal Democrat, and you know what a great stress that has been during my lifetime. [Laughs.] From the day I was seventeen I was racing deadlines, and I'm still doing that. I'm teaching a big course at USC, and in the summer I teach a course at the Idyllwild School of Music and the Arts in California. And I do a lot of public speaking. Just yesterday I was asked to prepare a speech for a conference in Las Vegas. And then there are panels and symposia and books.

I will say that at eighty-one, although I'm feeling pretty good, I'm well aware of the statistical menace of age. It is not a comfort to know that at my age I've already passed the anticipated life expectancy for American males. With that in mind, no matter how much joie de vivre I may have on a particular morning—even when I awake with a burst of energy—I'm aware there may be limited time for me. To the extent that there is less time, my need to create becomes sharper, keener. Also, there is the question of how long I will be able to perform at top form, to be able to perform effectively. In this sense, what the years do is rush the passer, to use the football term. I'm like a quarterback on the run, trying to get rid of the ball before I'm taken down.

I wish I could say that it is wonderful to feel busy and wanted and productive, and God knows I'm all those things, but sometimes I feel crowded by it. Pushed by it. It's been a lifelong situation, and at times I must confess that I have to wrench myself away from some projects and say to myself, "Now wait a minute, you haven't seen the kids for a week. Kate (my wife) would like to go out to dinner this week." I'm still struggling to find a balance in my life and I think it has to do with the "I'm not really growing old" syndrome. You stay busy to convince yourself that you're still young, still capable. You'd think that at my age you'd have sorted this out, reached a kind of balance, but I haven't. I'm not sure I ever will. But what I have to do is develop the capacity to say, "Now wait a minute. Do I really want to make this trip? Do I really want to make this speech?"

I guess there is a conflict in me between the need to be creative, the impulse to be creative, and the tendency to say, "Hey, I just want to listen to music, I just want to walk on the beach. Maybe I want to take a ride in the country. Maybe I want to make love." Don't rule that out. [Laughs.] Nobody should assume that when one has passed eighty interest in that department of life has eroded or disappeared.

One needs rest and fun time to get the creative juices flowing, to allow the right questions to surface. There is a very active principle involved in all creativity, and it's involved in imagination, and it's expressed very simply in two words: what if. What if I were to write a book about trivializing America? What if, à la Christopher Columbus, I got together some money and started an expedition? What if, à la Mr. Edison, I took some metal, some element, and made it white hot by an electrical charge? Would that create a new form of illumination? Fortunately, there is nothing that says that an eighty-year-old can't say "what if."

But I don't want to overrate old age. There are many sad things about growing old, and the literature of growing old can be very poignant. The worst thing about growing old is the erosion, the failing sight, the failing of the faculties. Having to use a cane. Being more susceptible to corrosive diseases—liver, kidneys, pancreas. Certainly all of those are not pleasant to contemplate. On the other hand, you reach instinctively for those models of successful old age, like Verdi, Shaw, and Michelangelo, who lived to be a good ripe age—you hold onto those models. It was Browning who said, "Grow old along with me, the best is yet to be." So it is not all dark chords. There is some brightness to it as well.

I think that the main thing that is to be cherished in growing old is dignity. Being able to do for yourself and not to be dependent on others. Unfortunately, the attitude in this society is that if you're old it is over. There are many countries where this attitude is alien. In the Orient old people are national treasures. But in this society our attitude is a little sickening, although I think we're coming out of it. The elders are asserting themselves now. The Gray Panthers are just a part of a huge general movement, of an awareness that senior citizens (I hate that term) have political clout and can exercise it. That they have rights.

There are times when I'm discouraged, when I'm down, when I feel that I never have amounted to anything, when I feel burned out. And in such times you might turn to your trophy shelf—you know, pick up a book you wrote or a well-done poem, go over fan letters, massage yourself with the awards you've won. But that constitutes looking back—and too much of that isn't healthy.

Since I'm on the subject of looking back, I remember now that the toughest birthday I ever faced was my fortieth. It was a big symbol because it said goodbye goodbye goodbye to youth. Even in the late thirties one still clings to the notion that one's a young man. It seemed to me to be calamitous to be forty, until, of course, I considered the alternative. But I think that when one has passed through that age it's like breaking the sound barrier. One realizes that it's not that bad on the other side. One slowly arrives at an accommodation, and that's part of the maturing process.

I remember at the age of forty-eight being asked by a student in North Carolina, "Have you thought about retiring, Mr. Corwin?" That absolutely threw me. I was staggered that he could ask that question; it was so far from my mind. But I've since had a softer reception to the term "retirement." And also one begins to have a softer and more accommodating attitude toward death. When you reach eighty, you begin to look at those

numbers . . . you realize that it could happen any day.
The poet Carl Sandburg and I were friends for many
years. He was a guest at my home for about a month one
time. (He was in his eighties then.) We were sitting at
breakfast one day and Carl was fishing in his pocket for
something, for a note that he had written. And I noticed
that he kept pulling out of his pocket scraps like lint—
they were little scraps of paper with things written on
them. I gathered some of them were quite old, because
you can tell how old a piece of paper is—the pencil
writing becomes a little obscured, the paper a little
brittle and yellow. And I said, ''What are those?'' ''Oh,
they're scraps of poems that I've been carrying around.''
''May I see them?'' I asked. He said, ''Sure.'' So I read
some of them. They were each three, four, five lines or
so. And they were beautiful things, little gems. ''Carl,
have these been published?'' I asked. And he said, ''No,
no.'' I said, ''But they're wonderful, why haven't they
been published?'' He said, ''Because I'm not through
with them.'' Well, now here he was, eighty. You see,
this is what I mean when I say ''staying in there.'' I don't
care how old you are, so long as words are in your mind
and in your heart and if there's thoughts and feelings
. . . there's no point at which the laws of nature say no
more writing, no more doing, no more living at ninety-
five.

You know, as a kid I couldn't wait for the cavalry to
come and for the big, loud finish. But as I've aged I've
become more tolerant and addicted to and eager to hear
the quieter passages, the softer, slower melodies. The
musical term ''andante'' literally means walking, in a

walking tempo. And when we get older we don't run anymore; we walk, don't we? Walking has its own mystique: it has a beauty all its own, a philosophy all its own. You can relate it to music—I remember reading about Brahms, who would take walks through the woods. One day somebody encountered him when he obviously had some great theme running through his head and there was a look of ecstasy on his face as he was walking. Well, how right that seems! I'm sure whoever walks all over God's heaven walks. They don't run. I don't think there's jogging. I don't think our heroes jog; I don't think God jogs. I think He's stately. I think He moves with grace, but always at a civilized pace. He's never rushing to get the 5:15 out of Grand Central, right? So God's a senior citizen too.

Norman Cousins

> ⤷ ⤷ ⤷ ⤷ ⤷ ⤷ ⤷ ⤷ ⤷

For thirty-five years Norman Cousins served as editor of Saturday Review, *but he was best known as "the man who laughed himself to health." His book* Anatomy of an Illness as Perceived by the Patient *was a best-seller. It describes the onset of his illness, in which his body became more and more rigid as the connecting tissue between cells broke down. During treatment he worked with his doctors, following their recommendations exactly. In addition, he began developing his own therapy, with his doctors' under-standing. He took carefully monitored doses of vitamin C and* complemented that with regular sessions of laughter. He watched film clips and television shows and read books on humor; the laughter then provided him with hours of pain-free sleep. Slowly he recovered. Today, in light of Norman Cousins's experience, many hospitals around the country offer similar programs of laughter as part of their total care plan.

Prior to his death in November 1990, Norman Cousins lived on the West Coast, where he taught a course to medical students at UCLA about positive emotions in healing.

I t never occurred to me that I would be planning for the later stages of my life when I came into this new community, the medical community here at UCLA. Rather, the feeling that I had was that as I was approaching the prime of my life it might be useful to put to work many of the things that had led up to this particular stage, and so I don't regard what I'm doing now as a prelude to retirement or senescence, but as almost a harvesting period. Pretty soon I do expect to be entering into the prime of my life.

I've never had a period in my life where I've felt more engaged than I am now, where I'm able to use as much of myself as I am now. I was at Saturday Review for a number of years, and a large part of my time was spent in presiding over interruptions. The correspondence would be very heavy, so the time for writing and sequential thought was rather limited. I loved Saturday Review and everything about it, but I discovered that in this new environment at UCLA the opportunities for sequential thought and writing are far greater and also more rewarding to me personally.

One of the things I have tried to do here is, first of all, make it clear that I would hate to have anyone think that I believe that you can ha, ha, ha your way out of a serious illness, or that laughter is a substitute for competent medical attention. I've always regarded laughter as a metaphor for the full range of the positive emotions, of which I would certainly include hope and faith and love and will to live, determination, purpose, and creativity. Laughter belongs in that general scheme of things, and laughter by itself helps—can even enhance—respiration. Some researchers believe that laughter helps to activate the endorphins, which are secretions put out by the brain that help to combat pain and also contribute to our sense of well-being. I don't know whether a scientific basis has yet been established for the belief that laughter can help activate the endorphins, but one thing is certain: the positive emotions can block the panic and the depression and the despair that all too often figure in the onset of disease or the intensification of disease.

Again, I don't think that we have to be clowns, but we do have to live a life in balance. A lot of us are starved for joy, and yet there's a lot of it out there; it's not going to happen automatically, but it's worth working for. You have to work at making joy. I go out to have lunch, for example, and joyousness is as much a part of my basic biological needs as food is, or anything else in life. I just program myself to be sure that I'm not shortchanged. And if my companions at lunch don't provide me with a laugh or two, I'm not going to pick up the check. [Laughs.]

When I first came into this new medical community at UCLA, I reached immediately for one of the medical textbooks to find out as much as I could about the human healing system and I looked in the index under "healing system." I found the other systems listed—the circulatory system listed as such; the autonomic nervous system listed as such; the autodigestive system or any of the body's systems, all having capital letters attached to their names, all specifically designed fields of study—but I didn't find anything under the healing system. That puzzled me. Of course, in the dictionary you had a listing under "healing," but not "healing system"— capital H, capital S. And I got to thinking about that and brooding over it, and then I realized that the way the human body heals itself is really not a well-developed branch of knowledge, either by the profession or by the person himself. Quite the contrary; we tend to take a rather mechanistic view of life, as though we're an automobile; we have a series of parts, and if anything goes wrong you fix the part or bring in a new part.

I think it's a mistake to feel that the only time the human body is going to be in a condition of repair is if you get the repair from the outside. Even if you must be treated by a physician, it's important for you to know that although you are not the doctor, you've got the mechanism of healing. And it's important to understand how this works. It's not a mechanical process, and it requires tending. We can't assume that you can ignore all the rules involved in maintaining a healthy system and not have something go wrong. It's equally wrong to assume that all you need to do is to reach for an aspirin or some other pill if something does go wrong. You have to have some connection between not just the knowledge of the disease, but why the disease occurred, why that breakdown occurred and what you do about it.

Illness is a natural part of life, just as birth is and as death is. It's unusual, indeed, to expect that we can get through this lifetime without some illnesses, even serious illnesses. But we haven't yet developed a philosophy of being able to deal with illness in this country. I think we're really educated to be hypochondriacs. We're educated to be very insecure about ourselves, so we tend to fall apart at the first sign of a problem.

I think we need a great deal of education. For example, people tend to believe that when they go to a physician with a complaint they're not getting their money's worth unless they also get a prescription. Well, the doctor knows that in eight or nine cases out of ten the body's going to be able to take care of its own needs. But the doctor also knows that the patient will feel that the doctor hasn't been listening or paying attention when the person describes his or her complaints, and so the prescription becomes the doctor's IOU that the patient's going to get well. But medications are medications, you see? When people become dependent on them, they run some risk. We've got to have more confidence in ourselves as a species, more confidence in our own robustness.

We're not going to live forever—no one gets out of this world alive—but the important thing is to get the best and the most out of whatever's possible. I think we can develop lifestyles that help us to get the most out of what is possible. There's an awful lot of fun out there. I think most people are starved for fun, and I don't think that our capacity for experiencing joy is being exercised to the extent that it should.

We've got to move beyond our limited view of what is possible. And we've got to educate ourselves so that the myths about health—especially those about health in old age—don't overcome our sense of pleasure and expectation. For example, there's always been the belief that the immune system tended to run down beyond a certain age. Well, research is now discovering that this plainly isn't true, that the immune systems of older people can, in fact, be at their ultimate because they've been able to come through so many problems. Biologically, therefore, nature works *for* us. But beyond a certain age many people feel that they're not contributing productively to society. They feel they've been liberated into nothingness and are a burden on others. Well, at that point you have a tremendous strain on all the body systems. But essentially and biologically it is being demonstrated that the immune system of older people can actually be at a high point. There really isn't a physical reason for these adverse expectations. Just as it becomes important to reeducate ourselves away from panic and away from terror about pain, so it becomes important to reeducate ourselves about the possibilities of life beyond a certain point. Once we change our way of thinking about that, there are physical changes that follow.

I myself have never had a period in my life where I've felt more engaged than I am now, where I was able to use as much of myself as I am. The word "young" is not especially appealing or magical to me. I don't know why we should be afraid of having lived a long time. I take a great deal of satisfaction, as a matter of fact, in reaching this point, and also in being aware of the fact that one of the benefits we get is that we're in a harvesting stage of our lives. We work all our lives to accomplish certain things, and then we reach the point where we can actually do the essential harvesting, and that is rewarding. I've always felt that the tragedy of life is not death, but what dies inside us while we live. And as the ancients have said, in and out of the Bible, choose life.

Roddy McDowall

Hume Cronyn and Jessica Tandy

⤳ ⤳ ⤳ ⤳ ⤳ ⤳ ⤳ ⤳ ⤳

HUME CRONYN: I don't want to end up with a smooth face.

JESSICA TANDY: Well, you're not going to. [Laughs.]

HUME: I haven't. I mean, the lines, the wrinkles . . . let them get deeper, particularly the laugh lines. That's not only what gives life its savor, but it's the thing that charges our batteries.

America's best-known married theater couple is now in their eighties. Separately and together, they have a long list of theater and film credits that have brought them awards and international acclaim. Jessica Tandy is best remembered for her role as Blanche DuBois in A Streetcar Named Desire *and for her most recent performance in* Driving Miss Daisy. *Hume Cronyn's work has ranged from* The Caine Mutiny Court-Martial *to* Death of a Salesman. *Together, they're known for* The Four-Poster, Foxfire, *and* The Gin Game. *You'd think that after over fifty years of a busy career they'd be ready to slow down. But as one journalist put it, "For the Cronyns, their best race is the one they haven't run yet."*

HUME: In 1959 I discovered I had a malignant melanoma of the eye and I lost the eye. It was really kind of small potatoes. It never caused me any great inconvenience. Thank God I never had a recurrence. At the time, I think it was useful to talk about it a bit on television and radio to other people who were going to face that. It's useful to be reassured about growing older, to hear what other people have to say about it—their fears, their anxieties. I have fears and anxieties in me that amount to anger about growing old. I don't see well. I have only one eye, but even if I had two I simply don't see as well. I don't hear as well. It infuriates me that I can't do the physical things I used to do twenty-five years ago. I've always been physically very active. I adore swimming, diving, spear fishing, water skiing, all that sort of thing. Can't do them anymore.

JESSICA: Oh, yes you can.

HUME: Well, I do them, but I don't do them very well. I can't do a fifty-foot free dive anymore. And there come days in your life when you think, "I know that tooth is going to come out, I have to call the dentist. I've got to get my glasses strengthened with another prescription. Why does my back hurt all the time?" God damn it, I'm getting older. I'm furious about it.

JESSICA: If anyone had said to me when I started, by the time you are eighty this will be your position in life, I would have thought, Wow, how wonderful. I never even thought I'd live to be seventy-five. And to still be active—why that was unheard of, because in those days a woman of seventy was thought to be remarkable if she could feed herself, almost. There are exceptions obviously, but people did age more quickly. I think we are able to keep active longer provided we approach our lives with creativity. I think the mere fact that we keep doing is self-creating. It's just flexing your muscles, that's what it is. I love to have time between work—when I'm vegetating and absorbing the world and so forth—but I'm happiest when I go back to work.

But if one is busy just for the sake of being busy, that seems very unproductive to me. Oh, life is full of that. There is an awful lot of work that is just the same thing over and over and over again, and you have to find ways to make it more interesting. I mean, if it's somebody who keeps a home going, there is a creative challenge in seeing to it that everyone is well fed and has a pleasant place to live. That's a very productive job, a very creative job; but if it's done in the spirit that "it's a bore," it will be unproductive.

I think one has to look forward to the future, but one also has to avoid repeating the same mistakes. We all repeat our mistakes over and over again, and we recognize that, and we say, "Damn it, I've done it again." But the wisdom, if that's what it is, or experience one has gained, it's in there and you can call on it and use it. The older you get, the clearer your life becomes. And I've noticed that more and more I'm beginning to see things from my parents' point of view, that I understand them more as I get older.

HUME: Do you understand me more?

JESSICA: Never. [Laughs.] You're an enigma, a lovely enigma.

HUME: I'm reminded of a few lines from a 1956 interview with the actress Enid Bagnold, in which she says, "How boldly we waste our time when we know there is so little of it. How we know nothing and would rather garden than think of it. How the slightest diversion makes one fling off the tedium of contemplating God. Life is wasted and flung away hourly in expectation. The days run by decoyed by it. Even getting up we expect breakfast. Then, there is Monday and Saturday and Christmas, there is a continual tiny date with activity. Or, if we are left in a pool of silence, let's cut our nails."

That's marvelous and embodies the whole threat of the waste of one's creative energy. You mustn't waste those precious energies; they must be used in a concentrated form according to the diminishing reserve of them which you have. And that takes some discipline and it's not easy to exercise. And if you don't exercise it, you are left in a pool of silence and the best you can do is cut your nails. I mean, one does think about that. Much of what we do has nothing to do with the creative process and everything to do with the normal abrasions of daily life. How often do you say, Okay, I'll give an hour to that, but the other hour I'll want for something that is truly creative, not just busy work.

There's something about our society, I think, that contributes to a point in one's life where you face deadly inertia. And it has to do with the pension fund, with Social Security, with reaching certain benchmarks of age. Sixty, sixty-five, whatever. This is the moment when I "retire." Then what? I mean, it's the unusual individuals and the admirable individuals who can continue to involve themselves in a way that allows them to continue to grow and stimulates what reserve of energies they've got at that benchmark age.

It all boils down to a matter of personal choice. I don't think one dwells on it until possibly you hit a very unhappy moment in your life when you find yourself in a state of suspended animation. This job's done, that's finished, my children have gone, and perhaps one of the worst things—I'm secure. Yes. And then what? The blood doesn't stop flowing through the veins, the creative juices—whatever they are—are still flowing and they demand being put to some sort of use. You need to try to continue doing those things that you find interesting, satisfying, self-fulfilling. For some it is gardening, for others it is knitting, for others yet it is reading.

But Jessica and I are very fortunate, very fortunate. We found ourselves doing something for which we had a passion and that passion has never abated. What has abated is the energy to continue it on the kind of schedule that we were once capable of. When I first started acting I could go out after a matinee performance and catch a movie and come back for the evening performance. And after the evening performance I'd go out, sit with my friends, drink, find a pretty girl, go dancing. Then I'd get up in the morning and take some exercise, go look at pictures in a museum, read a book—but no more. If I have a matinee, I come home and go to sleep. Then I go back and give the evening performance. And when that performance is over, I come home and go to sleep.

Jessica and I are lucky to have each other. It's tougher to do it alone. When you have somebody to share the problems and the joys with, the problems are cut in half and the joys are doubled. That's a real cliché, isn't it? But it's true. We are so lucky. We have had a partnership for fifty years, and we have always been there to support each other in the clutches. It makes an enormous difference.

JESSICA: That's why I think it's terribly important for people who begin their lives together to stick it out together. When difficulties come, whatever happens, they should strive to stay together because it will strengthen their relationship. Rather than throwing up their hands and saying, Well, I've got to change, I've got to get somebody else, people should remember that life is better for the shared troubles.

Something I'm forgetting is that laughter is absolutely essential in a relationship. To be able to laugh together is so important.

HUME: Jess is right. I mean, she's the laughter in the family. There are very, very few things that give me as much pleasure in the daily round as suddenly hearing Jessie laugh.

JESSICA: Laughter is a serious subject. [Laughs.] I remember an author who had written a play and he said that he found a scene that we were playing—one with sexual connotations—was funny to the audience. This distressed him greatly. He said, "Sex isn't funny." And Hume and I looked at each other and thought, "Where has he been?"

Laughter frees you up for growth. I think that the only way to keep fresh in your skills is never to be sure that you know how to do it. You can always learn new ways of doing things. If you are set in your ways and simply repeat things over and over, whatever you do will become stale and not only stale to your audience but boring to yourself. Each new project must be attacked as though it were a first effort.

HUME: I keep thinking of Samuel Beckett's most famous line, "I can't go on, I can't go on, I'll go on." I think that's partly what drives you, and also the awareness that terrifies us all, which is that if we stop we'll fall down.

JESSICA: I was just thinking right now that when I began acting, I was quite sure that I knew how to do everything. The older I get, the less I am sure I know how to do anything. Actually, I know more—I know it's there to be drawn upon. But I'm much less sure I know how to go about anything.

HUME: I don't share Jessie's modesty. We've led long, rich, artistically fulfilling lives. We're skilled in our craft, which is creative. I refuse to be modest about that.

JESSICA: It is an accepted myth that when people grow older they fall apart and don't do anything. I don't think that is altogether true. I think it is absolutely up to the individual. I mean, if you feel over the hill, you are over the hill. Each of us must do whatever we have a passion to do. It is our decision.

HUME: I'd bet that within the next decade you will find more and more senior citizens continuing to lead an active professional life—perhaps on a volunteer basis, perhaps on a continuing professional basis with a paid job and regular hours. But surely it's obvious, even simplistic, to say that if you don't continue to exercise, the muscles atrophy. And I'm not just speaking of muscles. I'm speaking of what goes on between the ears and the general enthusiasm for life. It's lovely and absolutely essential to rest at times, but if you say from now on I rest and that's my main activity, atrophy.

I'm going to digress one minute and tell you a little story about I. F. Stone. He retired about the age of seventy-two, or something like that, from journalism, in which he'd had a very distinguished career. Somebody was interviewing him and said to him, "But Mr. Stone, beyond this, what do you have to look forward to?" And he said, "I hope to die young, as late as possible." Isn't that a marvelous philosophy! And I think it applies to us. I wish I said it, instead of Mr. Stone.

I couldn't walk until I was one year old, and I'm coming to the end of the cycle now. It's inevitable, it's inevitable. You don't brood over it; you just hope the inevitable process of disintegration can be held off as long as possible. And the sum total of all that we're saying is, keep swinging. It's a lot easier to do when you are enthusiastic about what you're doing. And for those people who go through that terrible six months, a year, two years of loss, when they find that they are not simply alone, but horribly lonely, the strength of character it takes and the effort of will to keep involvement in life will keep them going and give them something to think of outside of themselves. The toothache, the back-ache, the bum eyesight—whatever it may be—is not easy to accept, but it's essential that you do. Absolutely essential. I haven't faced that yet. It scares me. I haven't faced it because I haven't had to face it. I can still write, I can still act, I can still swim; I can still do this, that, the other. Along with all my broodiness and complaints and bitchiness, I still am able to enjoy an enormous amount of what I do. Lucky, fortunate, blessed.

I suddenly think of melding two quotations. One I've already used in this talk, from Beckett, "I can't go on,

I can't go on, I'll go on.'' And add to that Shakespeare, ''With mirth and laughter, let old wrinkles come.'' I think I've misquoted it.

JESSICA: No, that's right. ''With mirth and laughter, let old wrinkles come.''

Ossie Davis

▷ ▷ ▷ ▷ ▷ ▷ ▷ ▷ ▷

Born in 1917 in Cogdell, Georgia, and educated at Howard University, Ossie Davis worked his way north in search of a career in acting. His first big breakthrough came in 1939 when he made his stage debut with the Rose McClendon Players in Harlem. Seven years later, in 1946, he made his Broadway debut in the play Jeb. *Over the ensuing years he secured for himself a solid reputation as a versatile and talented actor. He has starred in numerous film and television dramas, has produced and directed several of his own films, and has authored many biographies, among them*

Escape to Freedom: The Story of Young Frederick
Douglass *and* Langston, *based on the life of the poet
Langston Hughes. In 1989 he and his wife, Ruby Dee, were
named to the NAACP Image Awards Hall of Fame.*

A few years ago I was in a Broadway play that fea-
tured two old men who met at a park in New
York. One of the men is black and the other is Jewish,
and they're both seventy-six or seventy-seven. In the
play, with the help of the director, I had to achieve age;
I achieved it in my eyes, I achieved it in my hands, I
achieved it in my knees and how I walked and all. My
mama, who was ninety-one at the time, came to see the
play. Word got out during the intermission that she was
Ossie Davis's mother, so somebody looked at her and
said, "Oh, Mrs. Davis, Mrs. Davis, how does it feel to
look up there and see your son on stage?" And Mama
said, "Well, I guess it's all right, but I ain't never seen
nobody that old in all my life." [Laughs.]

My mother's still alive—she's ninety-three—and just
as vital as ever. She is a person with a great sense of
humor. She lives alone, at her insistence, and we call her
and visit often. She's a great storyteller and remembers,
vividly, things from her childhood and her marriage to
my dad and our growing up. She's just a wonderful
person to be around. And she dresses up sharp, you
know; steps out of the house togged to the limit.
[Laughs.] She has good taste and she gets enough money
from her children to buy herself nice things. I've never

seen her look like a "grandma" or an old woman, no
sir. And we love that about her. So, if I needed a role
model, Mom would be a good one.

I would say life comes a lot easier if you maintain your
sense of humor, no matter how old you are. I believe
that humor is divine; it's one of God's greatest gifts to
us. It enables us to put things into perspective and to
understand that we are very large and yet also very
small, and to make the adjustment, one with the other.
I grew up in the Depression as a child and I saw my
parents do things that, with humor, were extraordinary.
I was so glad when I ran across the story of Norman
Cousins in the hospital, seriously ill, and using humor to
regain his health. He got all the films of the Marx
Brothers and just laughed himself well. Now I under-
stood that. I can appreciate that laughter's good therapy.
It relaxes, it reduces; it does all those things and it keeps
you from going to jail or from going to a psychiatrist.

There is a most important reason why humor is so
vital to my life. I've always wanted to be a playwright.
I'm seventy-three, and I've written but one play. So I
can't afford to get sick and decrepit and die unfulfilled.
I have a strong reason to stay alive. And maintaining a
sense of humor is vital to helping me do that. Ruby also
has a strong reason to go on living. She has many, many
projects she wants to finish. We put off many things
because we were married, because the children came
first. So now is the time to do those projects, and Lord,
every day we check on each other. If I'm in Chicago and
she's in New York, we take each other's pulse by phone.
"How's the diet doing, how's your weight?" We buck

each other up in that regard. I love to eat and I was 235 pounds. And getting a liquid diet was horrid. I couldn't have made it, but Ruby and I went in together, so we would laugh at each other together and that sort of thing. And finally this morning I weighed 200 pounds. The doctor tells me my normal weight is 198, so I want to circle around that. Ruby and I understand that this is something we have to do for the rest of our lives, but we're ready. And humor is helping us through. We want to be healthy not just to be healthy, but because we have things to do. Common sense tells us that you've got to keep active to keep alive. I just truly believe that, and I'm more active now than I was at a younger age because I have more to be active about.

From experience, I would say that age is that point of elevation from which it is easier to see who you are, what it is you want to do, and from which you find yourself closer to the very center of the universe. Living through many changes, through many years, seeing many public passions rise and fall, gives you a sense of continuity. And that continuity not only is a part of your own view, but it also attaches itself to the continuity of time altogether. So I can look back and see way back, but somehow that enables me to look forward and see way forward. Age makes knowledge, tempers knowledge with experience, and out of that comes the possibility of wisdom. We never know if we're truly wise. We think the best thoughts we can. I think age gives you the possibility of thinking with less distortion—distortion that in the beginning was created by ego, by passion, by sex, by love, by ambition, by many things. And

as you encounter the distortions and as you go through
the periods in your life and correct them, they fall into
a certain pattern and you realize that the thing that you
thought was absolutely essential wasn't really essential at
all, it was a part of something else. And one thing led
to another, one thing led to another.

For example, getting married in 1948 I married into
a world that had a very definite definition of marriage.
I married into a man-oriented society, where the man
was the provider, the center, the whatnot, and the
woman circled around the man. But I married Ruby
Dee; Ruby had some other ideas about marriage.
[Laughs.] There were one or two other extra things on
her agenda that I didn't know about, but when they
came up I saw no reason to challenge her. For example,
after our first baby was born and we moved down to
Mount Vernon, New York, I remember Ruby standing
washing dishes one day and saying to me, quite confi-
dently, "You know, I'm not going to do this the rest of
my life." I said, "No? What are you going to do?" She
said, "Well, I'm going to be an actor. I'm still going to
act." I said, "Yes." She said, "I'm going to go to acting
school." And I said, "Well, okay." And at that time we
didn't have much money, so we decided that Ruby
would go to acting school and I would stay home and
sometimes wash the dishes and take care of the baby.
And when Ruby came home she would teach me what
she learned at the acting class.

Now, when I stepped into the marriage I didn't think
of that, but that happened. And over the years I think the
central thing that I've learned is how to more easily open

my life and let Ruby in. I think women are much more generous in letting people into their lives than men— although I might be wrong. I think that men come with a sense that they are the complete embodiment of what God intended should represent value, virtue, power, and all that sort of thing, and that women, to some degree, are there to service and serve them—that's how women fulfill themselves. Gradually, my wife and the circumstances of the time led me to a different under- standing, and I'm glad for that, because it made me a broader and a deeper and a much richer person. It has enriched my spirit, my spirituality.

I know that there is a material aspect of living that must be attended to, but I also know that the materials of the world cannot set the values by which the world must live. Science can deal with material, science can describe reality, science can tell you what is, but science cannot tell you what ought to be. Within us there is a need to define what *ought* to be, a need to know that there are other dimensions than the merely material. I think that's spiritual and I pursue that assiduously. I pursue it by being alive. I pursue it by writing. I pursue it by acting. I pursue it by listening to a symphony. I pursue it by going to church, by listening to a good sermon. I pursue it by taking a moral position about things, by committing myself to choices that are not easy. I have no embarrassment about understanding my- self as a spiritual person. It means that I am not jealous or competitive. It means also—and this is the best part of it all—that I learned a lesson a long time ago, and the lesson is, ''The way to make a man rich is to decrease his wants.'' I learn more and more every day what not to want and how not to want it. To me that is the regimen of the spirit.

It has to do with learning, but it also has to do with discipline, with putting yourself in perspective. It is the easiest thing in the world, for example, to patronize people, to put them off. You're tired, you've signed autographs, and people are asking you questions, some of which are absolutely silly. But you have to pull yourself in and listen, try to relate to what comes out of the person. And sometimes it is gibberish, sometimes it has no redeeming value whatsoever; but for your own benefit you have to listen and find out what is going on. That's why I question wisdom now as much as I ever had. I'm not content to tell you that now that I'm old, I'm wise. It is not that I am not in some instances wise or don't appreciate wisdom, it is just that I know that none of our knowledge is set; it changes from moment to moment. It is the person who continually questions his wisdom who has a remote chance of someday becoming wise.

So the aged are not necessarily wise, but chances are they are wiser than the young. And this is why I feel the world now needs us as it's never needed us before. In this age of rapid change in technology, somebody has to say, ''Whoa, technology can only affect reality; it cannot give you what should be, only change what is.'' Who's going to tell technology what should be? The people who've had more experience, and to have experience means you have lived through things.

I am coming to see, more and more, that my strength

and my power grows from my participation in the common strength and the common power of the people. That keeps me on track, keeps me understanding how wise I am and how wise I am not. You know, we need to have illusions of infallibility. We need to have illusions of power, we need illusions of "God damn it, we can understand everything." We need to have that, but we also need to understand that they are illusions, tricks by which we boost and help ourselves along. Ultimately, what we need is each other. There is one line from Gwendolyn Brooks that Ruby and I love to quote because we relate to it so much: "We are each other's harvest; we are each other's business; we are each other's magnitude and bond." Now that's a piece of wisdom—"we are each other." She could have stopped it right there.

Marc Raboy

Phyllis Diller

⪼ ⪼ ⪼ ⪼ ⪼ ⪼ ⪼ ⪼ ⪼

Time is running out. We used to live on borrowed time, but now we live on borrowed kidneys, borrowed hearts, borrowed livers. Now I'm even living on a borrowed face! I look better now than I have ever looked during my entire life—at least, for my age I look better, because I never looked like I wanted to look and now I look close to what I wanted to look like. The best plastic surgeons are artists, and some of them are sculptors. The man who did my first complete lift was a sculptor, a fine sculptor.

Zany, goofy, daffy, and ever so lovable, Phyllis Diller has been charming American audiences for more than four decades. In the 1960s she starred in her own television series, "The Beautiful Phyllis Diller Show," and appeared in several movies. During the Vietnam conflict she worked alongside Bob Hope to lighten the load of American GIs. All along, Phyllis Diller has been writing, writing, writing. Her many books include Phyllis Diller Tells All, The Complete Mother, *and* The Joys of Aging and How to Avoid Them. *She has received numerous national awards, as well as an honorary doctorate in comedy from Kent State University. She is seventy-four years old.*

I had so much fear planted in me by my mother in childhood that it almost paralyzed me, so I'm just glad to have made it this far! I was paralyzed with fear until way into my thirties. See, my mother was always afraid I was going to be kidnapped, although I don't know what for. I'm sure they would have brought me back, ha, ha, ha. There were always bank robberies going on around where we lived, so I just grew up with such fear. I was afraid of the dark, I was afraid of noises, I was afraid of bridges, I was afraid of authority, I was afraid of, oh, everything. I was just petrified all the time, because I had been taught so much fear so young. So growing old is a lot less frightening to me than growing young again!

Until I overcame my fears I could never have done what I've done. I have to give most of the credit to this one book, *The Magic of Believing*, by Claude Bristol. I was about thirty-five years old and I studied that book for two years. That book spoke to me personally. I immediately started experimenting with what he said to do, and I found that it worked. The two key words were "believing" and "magic." Believing *is* magic. You see, people don't get anywhere because they don't really believe they can. Before I read that book if I did anything and someone didn't like it, I was completely destroyed and I would stop doing it. Now, after I read that book, oh, baby. I mean, when I said, "I'm gonna do this or I'm gonna do that," they could have said anything and I wouldn't have paid a bit of attention. It may sound funny, but that's the name of the game. You absolutely must believe in yourself—you've got to believe that you can do it. You can't let fear and negativity run your life.

I don't hang out with negative people. I take out of my life whatever doesn't work, whatever isn't good, and people who are not happy people. I don't mean to say that if you get sick I won't speak to you again, no. I send cards to people who are ill and to shut-ins because I know how awful it is to be shut in. But there are a lot of people around you that bring you down, and you mustn't have those people around you. You must get rid of them, even if it's a spouse. I have watched women who wreck their careers by staying with negative men. Negativity kills.

I just don't believe in being sad. I don't think it's any good for you. Eventually it kills you, and of course it affects other people around you. When I was a little kid this song dropped a seed in my brain. It said, "Brighten the corner where you are." I learned that little song in kindergarten and I thought, Boy, what a great thing to do. So I guess that's what I do, show a little light. Comedy is about showing a little light.

No one can explain the thrill of hearing a lot of people laughing in unison. That is one reason why comics never die, they just live forever. Bob Hope is going to be eighty-eight in a few days, and I just went to George Burns's ninety-fifth birthday party. I'm booked to go and see George when he plays the Palladium at 100 years old. And, of course, Milton Berle is over eighty. It's the great life of hearing those laughs and being able to produce them that keeps these comics so healthy and so happy. I am absolutely certain that being happy is what keeps you young. I think that's how you do it: you have to find out what makes you happy and just hope that it's legal!

Look, I know it isn't always easy to be happy. It's very, very difficult for anyone at any age to keep a positive attitude. But a lot of it is letting go of your fear of change, allowing yourself to try new things. My secret to happiness in old age is to stay busy, to try new things. For example, I've been making great strides in my painting lately. Just last month one of my paintings sold for $4,000 at an auction. I'm really getting into it seriously because I simply love to do it, and it's nice for an older person to do. It's something I never had time for before because I had to build my fortune, take care of my children, get them through college—things like that. Now I have an actual chance to make choices, and that's why I took up painting. On my seventieth birthday I gave myself a studio; that was my gift to me.

I could never handle retirement. I mean, I couldn't do that. I don't understand it, unless you've had a job all your life that was very boring and you didn't like it ever and it was unsatisfying and you've been dreaming all your life about going fishing. But you see, I'm happy where I am and with what I do; it's so truly rewarding.

There are a great many joys to growing older. For one thing, you aren't as impatient as you were as a child. You don't throw an acorn on the ground and say, "Where's my tree?" You gain patience because you finally found out that things don't happen overnight. So you are patient with other people and you're patient with yourself. And you do gain wisdom and, hopefully, have worked out a way to live happily. If you haven't any wisdom and some real know-how by the time you get to be seventy, eighty, or ninety, it's been a real loss.

Hugh Downs

▷   ▷   ▷   ▷   ▷   ▷   ▷   ▷   ▷

Hugh Downs is one of American television's most visible personalities. He first gained national attention during the 1950s as the announcer and intellectual-in-residence on Jack Paar's late-night show. In the 1960s he was anchorman on NBC's popular two-hour morning program, the "Today" show. In recent years he has served as the host of ABC's "20/20" news program.

Downs's low-keyed, unflappable, erudite style accounts for his continued success. He radiates a sincerity and integrity that are rare on television. A man of wide-ranging inter-

ests—science, music, aviation, and painting, to name a few—he is able to share his curiosity and enthusiasm with his audience. Much of his time is now spent as chairman of the U.S. Committee for UNICEF, which he claims has given him the most satisfaction of all his avocations.

I've been interested in the subject of aging since I was thirty, when I was involved in a program that Jules Power produced for NBC called "How Long Can You Live?" It was really a geriatric medical special about the human life span—not expectancy, but span. It intrigued my interest in the whole idea of how long humans live and why we age and what happens when we age, and I formed a lot of ideas that I've revised slightly since then. At that time I would have thought that at my age now, which is seventy, I would feel old, but for some reason I don't. Now, people who've been injured, or who are ill, or who've suffered physical problems might well feel differently, but I don't think there's such a thing as feeling old.

There are advantages to growing old. For example, I'm deferred to at times as though I'm wiser by virtue of being older. And I suppose I am more wise now than I was when I was a young man. But the other side of the coin, of course, is that rampant in our country is the prejudice of believing that older people are not useful, that they're not as intelligent, that they don't have the same needs and, in some cases, aren't quite as human as other people. It's a terrible mistake for people to make the type of prejudice that bounces back because, with luck, it's a minority that we all join.

I've been fortunate because I've never suffered personally from somebody discriminating against me because I was older. There were certain reservations at times. I remember doing an aviation program where they thought that I had done a great job because I could do aerobatics in airplanes as well as younger people had done them, but they didn't realize that a younger person is more apt to pass out at certain G forces than an older person. There are medical reasons for this, and the Air Force knows this, but they thought it was remarkable that I could do these things. But actually I think as time goes on you don't gain greatly in endurance, although you can gain a little bit in intellect. In fact, as you get older, if your brain remains undamaged by injury or disease, your IQ can actually inch up; that's a more recent finding.

I don't know what it will take to turn around the American attitude. When will we finally understand that the older a person is, the more of a monument he is to what's worthwhile in life? Because all the forces that try to pull us down and destroy us in our cribs and through our childhood and through our mid-life are immense. If you survive those things, we still tend to put you in the same basket as decrepitude and impairment, which is not only unfair, it's kind of silly.

The way I see it, I finally got it together. It took me a long time, you know. Wouldn't it be nice if at twenty-one you had all the accumulated wisdom and acquired techniques that you later get? It just almost never happens. It makes me think that if I could contrive to live to be 400 years old, I really would have it down, wouldn't I? But you wouldn't suddenly want to become seventy years old, any more than you would really want to remain twenty. You know, there's an anomaly in our youth-oriented "Pepsi Generation" mentality. People say, "Well, what I'd like to have is the wisdom I now have, but in a twenty-year-old body." I think that's an anomaly because, first of all, to be twenty you would have to have the whole ball game—you know, the ignorance, the uncertainty. The other thing about being older is that I won't get killed in World War II—I already made it through that. I wouldn't want to try it a second time around.

I'm certainly to the point now where I know that the quality of life is far more important than the quantity of life. I'd rather die sooner than be overtaken by entropy to where my electrolyte balance wouldn't give me enough power to enjoy life. Death certainly doesn't hold any great fear for me. I feel a little like Woody Allen who said, "I don't mind the idea of dying, I just don't want to be there when it happens." I can understand that feeling, because I think if you remain true to what you want to be true to you won't have any massive regrets or guilt feelings; there's no reason that you can't accept the idea of your mortality pretty easily because you're just going where others have gone before and that's not necessarily a bad thing.

But now is the payoff, the icing on the cake, because even in my career I can do the things I want to do, rather than being handed assignments. I have some recognition now, and this is after a lifetime of working in broadcasting. And all of that is of value if you can cherish it and savor it. I'm not fighting anymore to arrive, because I *have* arrived.

You know, a man who was celebrated for his extremely good judgment was once asked, "How did you get so much good judgment?" And the man said, "Through experience." And then he was asked, "How did you come by the experience?" And the man said, "Through bad judgment." So that actually when you make mistakes, if you learn from them, that's fine. There is such a thing as getting in a kind of a rut where you keep repeating the same mistakes—you know, the compulsive, repetitive mistaker. That's a psychological problem; a normal person, I think, learns from mistakes. And I learned from mistakes right down the line—mistakes in career, mistakes in marriage—until I was finally able to say, "Boy, I'm out of that trap. Now I know the right technique."

The older you get, you find there's a tide that kind of goes out and leaves the rocks that are important. You see what are the big rocks and what are the little rocks. When you're younger, little rocks seem to be very large and they're not important, and the big rocks you can't even see. I think the older I get, the more I see that the big rocks mean keeping promises, keeping your word. And that's something to cling to, because there are some things in which I really feel like I would keep my word or keep a promise, even if it cost me my career or endangered my life. Your values become more important as you become older. If I were asked, for example, to push white supremacy on the air, I'd quit on the spot. I wouldn't say, "Oh, God, I've got to think about this. I've got to go talk to my wife about it and everything." I would simply say no, and if they said, "That's the end of your career," I'd say, "That's the end of my career." There are values that you put ahead of such things as career or money or anything else.

One of the better things that happened to me as I got older is that I finally arrived at a point where I realized you don't have to hate anybody. When I was very young I had a lot of hatreds that came from fears. Well, now there's nobody I fear, and therefore there's nobody I hate. That's a great freedom, because hate, as somebody said, is a weapon you wield by the blade and it just cuts you up. But if you don't fear, you don't hate. And there's a great liberty in it. Freedom is an amazing thing. I suppose that it's a cliché, but the price of freedom is responsibility. You know, if you're willing to assume the responsibility, you can really be free. You can't be free and still shun responsibility, or you wind up making phrases like, "I had no choice," or "My schedule won't permit," or "God won't let me do this," or whatever. To realize that you really are free and nobody can force you to do anything is a great blessing. For example, if somebody came into this room and said, "I'm going to kill you if you don't get out of the room," we would actually have many choices open to us. We could try to disarm him, we could sit here and die, or we could get up and go out of the room, which would probably be the wisest choice. [Laughs.] But to say we had no choice is nonsense, because we have the choice and we have the responsibility for making that choice.

Both Socrates and Freud stressed the importance of knowing yourself, because if you've got an awful lot of makeup underneath a level of your personality that you aren't conscious of, then you've got a dichotomy— you've got parts of yourself working against yourself. The more you know yourself, the more whole you are and the more comfortable you are and the more mature you are in the best sense of the word "mature." Not everybody matures, and that's sad. There are plenty of people who live to be quite old who don't mature. I liken it to a piece of fruit. You can go from green to rotten without ever ripening, and that's tragic. And there are humans that that happens to, so it's important to mature, to ripen. I suppose that's what I hope for for myself—that I continue to ripen until it's my time to go.

Julius Epstein

⧥ ⧥ ⧥ ⧥ ⧥ ⧥ ⧥ ⧥ ⧥

Julius Epstein has been a Hollywood screenwriter for over fifty years. His most famous movie is Casablanca. *But who recognizes the name Julius Epstein? Actors get fame and fan mail; even movie directors have names that are becoming famous these days. But the screenwriter? Even if he has attained success and made money, he lives in relative obscurity. Julius Epstein is eighty-two years old.*

It doesn't bother me that I'm practically anonymous. I am known among other people and screenwriters in the business, and by film buffs. As for the outside world, in fifty years I've written checks, signed credit card slips, and not once, not once, has a person said, "Julius J. Epstein; that name sounds familiar. Did you write . . . ? Have you any connection with the movie business?" Not once. I get the blank stare at all times. However, it doesn't bother me because I only want the respect of my peers.

It sounds like a cliché, but I don't feel old. Despite the pacemaker and the pill taking and the many visits and checkups at the doctors, I don't feel old. First of all, I jog about four miles a day over at the UCLA track. That isn't too bad. I'm ambulatory. But there are some physical manifestations of growing old. My hair isn't what it should be; I'm considering a hearing aid, glasses . . . little things like that. Yet I don't think I'm old, nor do any of my friends, my cronies. We don't think there is anything "old fogy" about us.

Take George Burns. He is ninety years old. He had a bypass a few years ago. At a party the other night he was the youngest person there. When I was a child on the east side of New York, my mother would pack up the three children and we would go to Rose Delancey and see the vaudeville. I remember being seven or eight years old and seeing George Burns on the stage. And now, seventy years later, he's just as fresh and energetic and vibrant. He's still the life of the party. He hasn't lost a single marble. So I don't think in his case age has done anything. On the other hand, some of my friends have Alzheimer's disease, so it's really like shooting crap. You have no control if you are going to fade mentally, or have Alzheimer's, or whatever. You just hope for the best and keep going as long as you can.

One of my little secrets is not to take anything too seriously. "This too shall pass." I don't think I'm engaged in a great art form, I don't think I made a lasting contribution to culture, but I think I've made a few people laugh. When I'm in the theater, in the movies, and the audience is laughing, it's a good feeling. But I don't feel I'm going down with the immortals.

You've got to have fun, you've got to live as you want to live. On my typical day, I'm up at six, and I spend about an hour or so massaging my gums while I catch the morning news. Then I get into a car and go to the UCLA track and run four miles. It consumes two hours. Then I come home, take a shower, and have a three-hour breakfast. I devour the entire paper. Then I go to work about noon, while everyone else is wasting time over lunch. Then I work for two hours, although not two hours on the clock. It might be two hours and eight minutes, two hours and three minutes, but my inner clock tells me my union hours are up. I feel that the law of diminishing returns sets in after that, and I begin laboring. I'm not a very disciplined person, but for a two-hour stretch I'm very disciplined. I figure that out of a twenty-four-hour day I can be disciplined for two hours. So two hours a day, a little nap, a visit to my grandchildren for an hour or so, and then it's time for the afternoon cocktail and dinner.

Being an elderly screenwriter is a tough business these days. It is so bad that the Screen Writers Guild has formed a committee to deal with the problems of older writers. I don't know what they can do about it. Years ago, a producer who is now old said, "I don't want anybody working for me who is over thirty-five years of age." And I guess that's true in a lot of fields. Look at colleges that have a mandatory retirement age. A professor can be brilliant at sixty-five, but he has to retire. He may be in his prime at that age. It is a severe injustice and a loss to the culture.

The very fact that I've initiated the last few pictures myself is proof of the seniors' dilemma. I've *had* to do that. Young writers are hired all the time, but they don't very often hire an older writer—practically never. The older people have survived by being entrepreneurs themselves. Those that couldn't adjust haven't survived. And survival is really a synonym for youthful. If you've survived, you are youthful. If you haven't survived, you're old.

If you go with the times, you're young; if you don't, you're old. As things change, you need to tell yourself that you've got to change along with them. It doesn't apply to me in music, because I can't stand the new music, rock and such, but aside from that I don't think everything was better in the old days. Pictures are better today, certainly our technology is better, medicine is better (which may be one of the reasons why I'm still here). So I don't think about growing old because I am not aware of growing old. I'm keeping up with the times. I haven't grown more conservative, or stodgier, or anything else. I only become aware of being old when people tell me I'm old. When people start helping me across the street it's a clue that something is happening.

And most photographs tell me that something is happening. I avoid looking at photographs—my mirror tells me all I need to know. Though it comes as sort of a surprise to me, my age is ripe. It's very ripe. I'm past the September song. But I never said to myself one day, I'm old. How can you say one day you are young and the next day you are old? It's such a gradual process. Really, people have to say to you, "You're old." I was kind of insulted when I got a notice from Social Security, "You are now eligible." But I didn't spurn it.

I know there is less and less time for me, that I should not put things off, but I do. Essentially, for want of a better word, I'm lazy. I'll do only as much as I can get away with. But the thought is there that there isn't much time left. You never know when, or how, so you better get to it. But I'm not getting to it.

M. F. K. Fisher

⨾　⨾　⨾　⨾　⨾　⨾　⨾　⨾　⨾

My only weapon in this whole world now is words, and I've spent my life sharpening that sword and I just hope that I can stab a few more things, slice a few more. It's an odd thing to realize that there is little time left. I feel extremely alive and alert and aware, and all my senses are going clickity-click, but I won't last much longer. I might last ten years or something; I might, but I rather doubt it. It's funny to know that you'd better say it before it's too late. I think that's one reason why people are rather rude when they get older. They want to say something, and it might not please everybody, but they may not have another chance.

"Writing makes me very happy," M. F. K. Fisher told me as we sat comfortably in her small house in the peaceful hills of Sonoma in Northern California. She lives quietly, in what might seem seclusion. Yet friends, fans, and family are constantly at her door. "My life is fun," she smiles. "I do what I want. I write, cook, and talk."

For most of her life, M. F. K. Fisher has been known to only a small group of admirers, among them W. H. Auden, who said, "I do not know of anyone in the United States today who writes better prose." Others have labeled her "the secret of the literary world." Some say she was the first to write about food with a literary flair.

Although she has written a novel, several short stories, and a variety of essays, the critics and the public all claim her revelations and insights, even her recipes, to be autobiographical. Now in her eighth decade of life, she continues to write, publish, and strive to improve her craft. "I want to write something good sometime, and I never have yet. To me I've not written well yet. I'm trying, I'm trying very hard, and it's rather frustrating to find that I'm eighty-two, which is chronologically toward the end of my life naturally, and I haven't done it yet. I don't want to write War and Peace; *I just want to write something that I like, and I haven't done it yet."*

One thing I resent about being older is that I don't have the physical energy to cope with all the things that I want to get on to paper. I've always been that way, though, racing my own inner deadline. No pun intended; it's sort of macabre at this point in my life. But it is an inner deadline, really, and I'm not quite meeting it because there's so much to say and only I can say it. That's what I feel inwardly.

Outwardly, I think I put up a pretty good show. My hair is fine and I take good care of my skin. And I like to wear a little makeup. I stand up straight, even though right now I hobble a bit because I have Parkinson's disease. I suppose that for the past ten years I've walked in a rather stiff, gingerly way, but I walk standing straight up. I have a certain dignity in my presence, I think. And I like to smile and laugh, although I don't do it unless I think that something is worth it. I'm curious. I have good manners. I know how to be polite and thoughtful to people older than I, if there are any around.

My husband told me that every self-respecting woman must have a full-length mirror in her house to see herself from top to bottom clearly. My full-length mirror is facing me at about a distance of ten feet from my bed when I get up in the morning. For decades I've slept without any pajamas or a nightie on, except in hotels and stuff. And about a year ago I suddenly realized that I could not face walking toward myself again in the morning because here is this strange, uncouth, ugly, kind of toadlike woman . . . long thin legs, long thin arms, and a shapeless little toadlike torso and this head at the top with great staring eyes. And I thought, Jesus, why do I have to do this? So I bought some nightgowns. I felt like an idiot, you know. [Laughs.] But I couldn't face it in the mornings. And I got some rather nice-looking gowns. My sister, Nora, has always worn beautiful lingerie, and she thinks my nighties are just abominable. If I'm going to hide myself, I want long-sleeved, high-necked, to-the-ground granny gowns. [Laughs.] I'd much rather not have to wear them, but I will not face that strange kind of half-humanoid, half-toad walking toward me in the morning. [Laughs.]

I don't mean to compromise with the gowns and all, and I don't think I'm a compromising person, but I certainly do know that there are certain facts of life that you've got to accept. I know some women who refuse to be old and they are like zombies walking around. They are lifted here and lifted there; you know, altered in the nose and eyes and chin, and they can't smile because it would ruin their latest do. In Japan there are a great many women who have their eyes unslanted. It's okay if they feel better, but I think they are compromising their fate and I refuse to do that. That's all, I refuse.

One of the nice things about growing older is that I am much less bound by conventional behavior than I used to be. For instance, if I want to wear slacks, I don't give a damn. I really am going to wear pants, which just isn't done by women of my age and generation. But who cares. I'm going to wear them since I have a hip ailment and it's awfully hard for me to put on panty hose. I now wear maternity stockings, something that goes up to my knees. I think old women's legs are not pretty. I like pretty legs. Some old women have beautiful legs, but I don't—now they're kind of old chicken legs. [Laughs.]

And so I'm going to wear slacks. Tough.

If I thought every day about being old, I'd go crazy. But it's not oppressive at all. It's a condition and I accept it. The only thing I regret is that it's the last one I have to cope with. And obviously I regret at times that I have practiced so long how to write as well as I could now that there's not an awful lot of time left to do it in. I know there are a great many things I never will say or do, and I'm sorry about that. The fact is that I will not let it depress me. I mean, I could just put my head in my hands and say, Oh God, my life is over, there's no use going writing any longer, there's very little time left and whee, let's go off to Paris or something. Well, I would if I wanted to, but I don't. I really like to stay pretty much as I am. I love being with the few people I like. I think that's important. It's more poignant and important when you know it may be the last time I may see you. You are very keen in my mind, and as long as I have a mind you will be. And I think that's true of even drinking a cup of milk or something. Old age brings a special kind of sensitivity, a special kind of intensity to things.

When I think of some of the things that I used to do when I was younger, I'm amazed. I could not possibly do them now. But, of course, there are things I can do now that I couldn't do then. For one thing, I can concentrate more and I enjoy things in a way that I never did before. As an older person, I feel, for instance, the color of that strange flower at the end of the table more intensely than when I was younger, although I was very aware of it when I was younger. I like it very much.

This afternoon I look forward to lying down. I didn't sleep enough last night, and I don't plan on sleeping this afternoon. But you know, half horizontal for half an hour and I'm okay again. When I was younger I didn't need a nap, but so what? I can revive; I revive very quickly, like a desert plant with just a little bit of water.

I appreciate very much being alone now. In fact, I plan it. I hoard moments of being by myself and kind of charging my batteries. I think you are more aware that as you get older, you have to charge them a bit, deliberately, instead of just counting on unlimited electrical energy.

I'm jealous of my time. For many years now I have contrived and planned and schemed and tricked and everything else, and been a bitch about it, but I like to spend Christmas day all by myself. I have many happy years of Christmas from my childhood, but now I'm jealous of any impingement, any infringement on my privacy. And I have a kind of ritual which is so refreshing to me that I'm like a new person. I'm looking forward to it right now, as a matter of fact. I can hardly wait for Christmas. It sounds silly, but on Christmas day I just pull up the drawbridge. I lie, I tell people I'm going away. I'm not going away—I'm going to be right here. But I have a bottle of very good champagne, properly chilled, and I open it up in the morning and I drink it all day—just little nibbles, all day long. And I eat what I want to eat. Something kind of silly, usually. I like to drift around, and all day long I play music—records I haven't heard for maybe ten years or two months. Whatever I want, all day long. I don't turn on the radio.

I don't read much. I empty drawers and drift around and write a little bit, take a little nap in the morning if I wish, lie down, snooze, eat a little bit of, let me see, smoked salmon on a matzo cracker. It's just a complete self-indulgence. And I awake the next day as if I were a brand-new person.

For a long time in my life I thought I would go to Greece to live and die. And then sometimes I thought I would like to go back to Aix-en-Provence, but I can't live where I want to live and couldn't live the way I have to live because I'm crippled, handicapped. Since I can't do it, here is the best for me. It's a put up or shut up job, you know. Fortunately, I could at least choose that much. There are many other choices that have been open to me and I've chosen this one. But I really don't think you choose too much. It's kind of chosen for you, I think. An awful lot of life is by chance, and you make the best of it or you don't.

I would really like, in my last years—which I know these to be—to leave an impression of a mild enjoyment and tolerance and courtesy. I think courtesy is a great thing. Just the innate courtesy, not the manners that one uses to stand up, sit down, all that stuff. But just a real innate courtesy that is nice, not demanding about any-thing, belching or scratching or something. I'd like to be rather graceful about my last years.

And just as young people are all different, and middle-aged people are all different, so too are old people. We don't all have to be exactly alike. This thing of saying, "Well, he's an old man, he's old now," in which he's put into a certain drawer or category, that's not true at all. There are all kinds of old people coping with a common condition, just as kids in puberty when their voices start cracking. They all have to deal with this problem, but they are all different. Every one of them is different. We old folks get arthritis, rheumatism, that sort of thing; our teeth fall out, our feet hurt, our hair gets thin, we creak and groan. These are the physical changes, but all of us are different. And I personally feel that you follow pretty much the pattern of your younger years. I think that some people are born young and some people are born old and tired and gray and dull—quite often dull. You're either a nasty little boy turned old man or a mean little old witch turned old or an outgoing, free-loving person turned old.

As for myself, I feel very excited about life and about people and color and books, and there is an excitement to everything that I guess some people never feel. I feel sorry for them. I have a lot of friends who are thirty-year-old clods. They were born that way and they'll die that way. They never sort of grow up or grow down or learn or do anything. But me, I'm happy, I'm alive, and I want to live with as much enjoyment and dignity and decency as I can, and do it gracefully and my way if possible, as long as possible.

Burl Ives

≫   ≫   ≫   ≫   ≫   ≫   ≫   ≫   ≫

B efore I was born I'm certain that I was fashioned to sing, and to sing simple songs, because I went to church prenatally and my parents sang in this simple little church. They sang all these wonderful evangelistic hymns that are very dramatic, poetic, and exciting. What I'm talking about is folk poetry, pure religious folk songs, the basic four-part hymn from which the Hawaiians got their folk music and from which black people got their spirituals.

Outwardly, Burl Ives looks very much as he always has. Large, robust, an imposing presence with a thick beard and sparkling eyes. His seventy-five years show gently with some wrinkles and white hair. When he isn't performing to appreciative and enthusiastic audiences, he lives a quiet and secluded life in the mountains near Santa Barbara, California. Together with his wife, Dorothy, he enjoys a life of contemplation and introspection.

This whole matter of growing old has a great deal to do with one's frame of mind. The mind controls the whole business; the mind controls the heart of the matter, you see. If your mind says, "I'm old and crippled," you are. If your mind says, "I'm not going to give in to this arthritis or to this stiff neck," then it goes away. It's largely a matter of thought; you make your own reality. I believe that very strongly. If you want to be depressed about the world, that's fine—you can do that—but that will only drive you right down there with everybody else. Soon you'll be looking to alcohol and drugs to find relief.

The difference between me as a young man and me as an old man is all a matter of attitude. No, not attitude—intent; intent, that's a better word. Twenty years ago I liked to go to nightclubs in New York and have people come up to me and say, "You're Burl Ives, the great performer." Much of my earlier life was spent seeking that kind of external gratification. But that's not true today. You see, about twenty years ago I began asking questions: Who am I? Where am I going? What is the significance of life? What is my purpose here on earth? Those are the sorts of questions that captured my attention. I became more and more introspective. So I'm less social now and more philosophical about life than when I was younger.

Material things have become increasingly less important to me as I've aged, while spiritual things have become more important. I remember back in 1946 when I ran into tax problems and had to sell my home and four-acre property here in California. Friends came to me weeping, telling me that this was a terrible thing. But I recognized even then that the house and the land were really only on loan to me, that a man isn't here long enough to truly say that he owns anything. So I just said to my friends, "I'm just passing through. Don't fret about this; something else will come along." I lost something that appeared to be very important in order to gain something far more significant.

Along with the loss of that house came a new approach to my performances. In the old days when I went out in front of an audience, for instance, at a nightclub or concert, I went out with the idea that I'm going to "put it over on the audience." I had a planned walk onto the stage, I had a planned set of songs, and I even planned what I was going to do with my face—when I'd crack a joke and such. It was as well planned as a good bank robbery! Well, it was all contrived. The only time it wasn't was when I started to sing, because something else took over. And that something was a form of God-given inspiration, and the audience could sense that.

Now I'm smart enough to know that the only time I can sing effectively is when I bring my mind into a state of innocence. When I am in a state of innocence, I can walk on the stage feeling confident that people will enjoy my performance. Now I just go out on the stage; I'm not worried about anything. I've got but one purpose, and that's to touch the hearts of as many people as I can. I let myself go into the feeling of my music and trust that my audience will feel that too.

I think that as someone grows older he doesn't worry so much about what the outside world thinks of him. He realizes not only that it is a waste of time, but that it impedes his enjoyment of life. I'm reminded of a story that my great friend John Steinbeck once told me. He was coming down from Sag Harbor, New York, on the train, and sitting in front of him was a young lady and her tweedy, pipe-smoking grandfather. All the way down the coast this young lady was yak, yak, yakking, talking her head off about other people and what they thought of her. When the train finally stopped in New York, the old man took a puff on his pipe and turned to the young lady and said, "You wouldn't care so much about what people think of you if you realized how little they care." And I think that's what happens when one gets older; we are smart enough to know that, or at least we ought to be. [Laughs.]

I think my life has been a long, slow process of trying to move closer and closer to the spirit by moving closer and closer to the heart. I'd like to believe that as I've gotten older, I've gotten smarter. I figure if a person doesn't get smarter, he's doomed. I'm certainly happier now; I have more fun now. I know now that I can do without all the material whoop-de-do that most people think is so important. That is not life. I know that.

The heart is what's important. It all comes down to a vibration of the heart. Our hearts are the eternal part of us that goes on and on. I feel very strongly that I am a part of the entire cosmos, that I'm not something apart from the life of this pulsing universe. I am an integral part of it. And I suppose that's why I'm not at all afraid of death, because I see that my life is just a matter of growth and change. Everything is changing and creating at the same time. You see, I think disintegration is creativity. That might sound a little like Lao-tzu, but I think he was right. Everything is in the process of change. The way I figure it, when I die I'll simply be changing a raincoat, moving on to another level of energy, because I'm confident that energy never dies. If a piece of wood will never die, this bouncy thing called Burl will never die as well. Walt Whitman once wrote, "Out of the ocean, endlessly rocking." He referred to the Great Mother endlessly rocking the ocean, and that rhythm is pulsing in all things. Everything has a rhythm. As another man said, "The longest journey any man will ever take is from his conscious mind to his heart." So the older we get, the more we grow into life, the more wisdom we obtain, and the closer we move toward the rhythm of the Great Mother "endlessly rocking."

There are times when I'm not so confident, I admit. Sometimes I look in the mirror and say to myself, Now, here is a ridiculous character. That's me? That old coot with the beard and that funny look in his eye? Is that me looking at me? There's a moment of hilarity there that is pretty wild. But all great comedy is a double-edged sword, so that the other side of that hilarity is the sad old face. John Steinbeck once wrote about somebody who saw the great eye of a Chinese man, and as he entered the eye he found the whole suffering world on the other side of it. So if you look into yourself deeply for any period of time, you begin to see yourself and your follies and the follies of the world. You also begin to see yourself passing on, see yourself dying. At this point I say to myself, I am not the body, I am not the mind, I am not even my emotions. I am spirit itself. When you can put your finger on that you can laugh again, because there is something remarkably freeing and joyful about the fact that every single one of us is spirit. I always end up with a little ancient prayer that goes like this: "Oh hidden life, vibrant in every atom. Oh hidden light shining through every creature. Oh hidden love embracing all oneness. May each who feels himself at one with thee know he is therefore one with every other."

I can't get up as fast as I used to, and I sure wouldn't be able to run much of a footrace, but I figure I'm a little like old Tom Paine. It seems that when Tom Paine was a very old man one of his political rivals met him on the street and began to chide him. "Well, Tom Paine, I guess you're about through now, aren't you? You're crippled and you can't see. Tom Paine is nearly finished. It won't be long now." Tom just looked up and said, "Oh, you're quite wrong, sir. I admit that the roof of my house leaks in the wintertime and that my house is very cold. And some of the doors do need fixing and some of the windows are missing. But there is nothing wrong with Tom Paine.''

Elizabeth Janeway

≫　　≫　　≫　　≫　　≫　　≫　　≫　　≫　　≫

Elizabeth Janeway has long been considered a leading spokes-person for the women's movement, although she is hardly what one would call a strident feminist. Over the years readers have been strongly attracted to her work because she draws upon her experiences as a wife, mother, and working woman. Her many highly praised books include Between Myth and Morning: Women Awakening *and* Powers of the Weak. *She lives in New York City with her husband, the economist Eliot Janeway.*

I'm seventy-seven. I was born in October 1913, just a few months before the First World War. One of the things I remember is that I was taken to a parade of returning soldiers and I was simply having fits over it because my mother said I had to wear a coat I didn't like. I do remember the parade a little bit, and I remember the great flu epidemic, because my father caught it and got himself home from New York to Brooklyn where we lived and got his key in the door and turned it and fell into the front hall. And when we got him to bed there was the problem of keeping the cats and me out of the room. These early memories that I can go back to are simply the product of how old I am.

There are a lot of things that call attention to the fact that I am growing older. One of them is the fact that people who were important historically and whom I knew are not so well known any more. So sometimes people say, "Huh," if you mention this or that person. I'm not bemoaning any of this. To have had a long and happy life, and to have published fifteen books, and to have been head of the Author's Guild Council and of the New York Council for the Humanities, and to have lectured all over the country, as I have done, has been a wonderful life. I'm not going to sit and moan over the fact that not all those things are happening now. I do a fair amount of traveling and talking, and I still continue work with some organizations, and I plan to go on writing.

One of the great things about writing is that nobody tells you to retire until the public does, so there's no age for it. Writers and players, performers, musicians, can go on into their seventies and eighties. Bernstein, Pierre Monteux, and Stokowski went on conducting into their eighties and nineties. So it's a wonderful thing if you're self-employed; it's a blessing.

I think a very hard thing for people who are retired is the break and the change in life. The shock of being retired, I think, must be very difficult. And I notice that some of the magazines for older people are so god-awful cheerful all the time. "Isn't retirement wonderful. Now you can go and climb the Alps," is sort of the attitude. Well, it's too bad that we can't enjoy the Alps when we are younger. Why do we have to wait until we are retired to enjoy life? The world isn't geared to it, pension plans aren't geared to it, Social Security isn't geared to it. I suppose the Alps are okay, but I figure I'll go on writing as long as anybody will print it in the hope that posthumously my voice will be heard. It's a joy to me to do what I do, and I think I am very, very fortunate. I feel blessed I'm not retiring from a nasty kind of work that I really hated and then going out and having a fun time on Carnival Cruises or something like that. If you are looking at a definite retirement age, I think you ought to plan more than a cruise or two.

I find solace in activity and working with people, and I think anything you can do to help others is marvelous. I think people who work with the churches, for instance, are doing great things. I'm not particularly religious myself, but I think there's an enormous amount of social work that can be done that way. I think any voluntary work that keeps you active and part of a process, an ongoing process, and involves you with people who are different ages, is wonderful. If you can continue in a professional organization, like my involvement with the Author's Guild, you are lucky. Since I was once president I'm on the board forever, and I do go to most of the meetings. At times I function as their back file of what happened in the 1950s, so it's handy to have me around. I can say, "We tried that back then, and it didn't work then and I'll tell you why."

One of the things I've noticed about getting older is that time telescopes. I can remember quite clearly, for example, the moment when I fell over Franklin Roosevelt's feet on a raised podium while an Irish tenor was singing "When Irish Eyes Are Smiling" up at Hyde Park. And that memory is something that lingers very clearly. Roosevelt reached down and put one big hand under my elbow and just picked me up. He was, of course, very powerful in his arms and shoulders from hauling himself around on those crutches. That is so vivid in my memory that it could have happened yesterday.

I think I value the experience I've had. I don't mind talking about it. If people are willing to listen, I'm always happy to tell them something that I think would be of use. I was out in California at a conference, for example, and one of the speakers talked about a writer whose work I had read a great deal of, and one of the phrases that he used was misinterpreted and she didn't know how to explain what it was he'd meant. So I leaped up and explained what it was he'd meant, and everybody, including the speaker and the people at the back, were pleased and thanked me afterwards. That's what I mean by using one's experience in a good way, when it can be useful. Older people who have experience should feel able to say something like, "Do be just a little careful about this here."

I would be lying if I didn't admit that I'd rather be younger. I would certainly rather have more experience ahead of me than behind me, because I love this world, in spite of the horrible things that go on. I think there's such a potential for joy right here that I can't say I wish I wouldn't live longer. I take such great pleasure in events and things these days, take so much pleasure from friendships, from walking in the park with my husband, that I focus very little on the past. I love seeing the spring come back, and I would hate to spoil it by moaning over what I did or didn't do in my lifetime. Any worrying I do now is about what I'm going to do next, not about what I did in the past, I promise you. I only wish I could stay a bit longer.

Marty Knowlton

⧓   ⧓   ⧓   ⧓   ⧓   ⧓   ⧓   ⧓   ⧓

In the autumn of 1974, Martin P. Knowlton—student, teacher, research engineer, backpacker, world traveler, and social activist—together with his old friend David Bianco, created the American Elderhostel* system, a nonprofit network of universities and other social service organizations dedicated to serving the educational needs of older adults. The Elderhostel program has grown steadily ever since, with

*For more information on the Elderhostel program, write to Elderhostel, 75 Federal St., Boston, MA 02110-1941.

more than 220,000 Elderhostel participants each year.

Marty Knowlton is now a seventy-two-year-old poet and wandering mendicant. Occasionally he is found daydreaming at an American Elderhostel program.

Shortly after I returned to the United States from a four-year stint in Europe, I went to visit a friend and former colleague, David Bianco, who had since become the director of residential life at the University of New Hampshire. (This would have been around 1973 or 1974.) David immediately took me under his wing, even though he announced that it was questionable whether I could ever be rehabilitated; this old man who'd come back from four years of backpacking in Europe had long white hair and a beard. But he decided that he would have me work as the manager of the small youth hostel they set up every summer on the campus of UNH. During that summer I just became more and more conscious of the plight of some of my ex-colleagues who had retired and who were terribly, terribly unhappy in retirement. In particular, these were people who feared deeply that as they grew older their minds would degenerate. I was astonished to discover that almost everybody believed that; it never occurred to me to think that. One day I told David some stories about the wonderful older people I had known in Europe. Well, David got very excited about these stories and hammered his hand down on the table between us, saying, "Oh, my God, we shouldn't be running a youth hostel, we ought to run an elder hostel.'' So that is how the elder hostel movement began in the United States.

The idea of bringing together thoughtful seniors wasn't new—it had been tried before—but somehow it had never worked. The important thing about Elderhostel was that we held on to the idea long enough to discover elder hostelers, and my God, it was true; there were many stimulating and exciting seniors out there dying to meet one another. Not only doesn't your mind begin to fail automatically, it goes on getting better. And elder hostelers are the most apt demonstration of this that you can find anywhere. It turns out that there are thousands—*hundreds* of thousands—of these thoughtful and creative elders.

Well, the Elderhostel program grew with such rapidity that I had to leave it. I wasn't pushed out; I just wasn't a very good organizer—and I knew it. I'm now living the life of a gypsy, and it seems to suit me rather well. Right now I'm living at a youth hostel at Fort Cronkite in the Golden Gate National Recreation Area, and I have an office in the national park. I'm running an organization called Gatekeepers to the Future, which deals with the same population that Elderhostel does, people who are, as we call it, ''retirement age.'' And we ask them if they will consciously and seriously accept the responsibility of becoming agents of the future, of becoming representatives for the disenfranchised people of our democracy and the people who haven't been born yet. That involves studying what's happening, the impact that we're having on the future, and trying to understand this effectively so that we can moderate the negative effects we're having on the future. The people of retirement age in the United States own something like 70 percent to 75 percent of the wealth of the country. And they have this incredible voting behavior that makes them have true political impact way beyond their numbers. Whatever is happening in the way of the formulation of public policy at the present is going to affect the lives of people born twenty-five, thirty, forty, fifty years into the future. So we're the ones that are in charge, really; it's our responsibility. We are the gate-keepers to the future.

I'm excited about Gatekeepers, but I must admit that I've had a bad patch in the last few months—high blood pressure problems and an assortment of other physical ills. I think I have a tendency to take things too seriously and I really was grief-stricken by the Persian Gulf War; the war was just devastating to me. I saw it coming—I could've plotted the scenario almost to a T—and I just felt totally helpless. It was a terrible, terrible, wrenching kind of time that made me sleepless, tense—all kinds of things. But I'll bounce back, as I've done so many times before.

I find my values these days to be simple to the point of simplemindedness. In many ways, I'm still a little boy who believes in the Golden Rule—fundamentally, that's still my belief; it's what jerks my chain, you might say. Somewhere fairly early in my life—say, in my thirties—I became aware of the fact that I was doing things and acting in certain ways purely for the purpose of earning more income, and I did not like that as a motivation. Gradually that became an itch that I needed to scratch. That was what finally prompted me, in the spring of 1970, to give away everything I owned. I then took $600, a backpack, a little two-man tent, a lightweight sleeping bag, and an extra pair of sneakers and went to Europe. I wandered around Europe for four years and came back to the United States with $600 and a thirty-pound backpack; it was a great, great, great experience. I lived literally free of the sense of doing anything for money. When I worked at all, I worked as a pick-and-shovel laborer on archaeological sites. My pay was twenty-seven dollars a week for a forty-eight-hour week, and I loved it; it was just a fantastically good time of life for me and a way of getting myself back on some kind of track.

To me, I'm living better than the traditional American dream. I have a total income of $600 a month, and that's Social Security and a VA stipend. I probably give away an average of $200 a month because I don't need it. I literally end up every month with money to spare, and still I do everything I want to do. I really have a life of complete freedom because I refuse to work for money, and when you refuse to work for money you can have damn near any job you want. I just don't have a high level of material want—and part of that comes from the training I gave myself from 1970 to 1974. Since then I really have not had any particular money motivation. I started Elderhostel and didn't pay myself at all for a year or a year and a half. My total income from Elderhostel in the first three years was probably under fifteen thousand dollars. But it wasn't a conscious thing of saying, ''I'm going to deny myself something.''

I never denied myself anything that I wanted. My life-style, my needs, my satisfactions were just coming from a different kind of place.

Most people would hate to have to give up all of their tapes and books and so on to live the way I do, and it wasn't easy for me either. I gave away a library—a fairly extensive library—in 1970. And I gave away another burgeoning library in 1982. But, hey, it's just books, and books are just another kind of possession—if you let them, they will own you. I confess to moments of rue that I no longer have a Webster's unabridged dictionary, and I wish that my way of life allowed me to carry around a few reference books that I don't have, but hey, I get all of my books from the public library. One of my regular recreational expenses is library fines. The library treats me very kindly—they ignore a lot of my violations and don't fine me anywhere near the degree I should be. There are things I'm tempted to cling to, but the only things I do cling to are these hundreds of poems that I have. That's my only baggage. I have no particular desire to publish my poetry, but I enjoy it, I love it, I like to read it, it makes me cry sometimes. It also is a way of literally reidentifying myself, or identifying myself for the very first time.

I like being an old guy. I'm much more secure in who I am. There's been just huge amounts of thrashing in my life, but I've learned to reflect on them, to learn from them. You know, there's no way that one can ever change the past. So when I talk about having lived through unsatisfactory and disturbing episodes in my past, there's nothing I can do about those things. All I can do is understand myself and recognize that virtually all of the bad things that have happened to me in my life, as far as I know, were things that I could have changed. As long as I keep recognizing that, it's useful to me because I'm now less ready to hide myself behind circumstances and say, "Well, I can't do this for this reason or that reason." I usually know where responsibility lies now, and I'm much more ready to act in a responsible fashion than I have been. I'm growing up. But, my Lord, if regrets were snowflakes I'd be buried right now. As a matter of fact, they might have even formed a glacier by this time.

I really think that I'm more strongly in touch with the realities and much more deeply in touch with the unrealities as an old man. Many of my sensations of living are almost blindingly vivid now. I love being alive at age seventy-one. I anticipate loving it just as much, maybe better, at seventy-two. I describe my function today as "stirring things up." Now, it isn't something that I do consciously, and I try to be cautious when I realize that I'm being disruptive—I don't want to send somebody into hysterics or anything like that. But on the other hand, I'm perfectly pleased with myself when I have the sense that I have stirred things up; that's living. If you're not stirred up, you're not really living. Elders need a certain amount of discomfort to really live; they need irritation, okay? They need to be indignant about things. By God, if you can't be indignant, you aren't anything.

Katharine Kuh

≫ ≫ ≫ ≫ ≫ ≫ ≫ ≫ ≫

The illustrious Katharine Kuh served as the first curator of modern art at the venerable Art Institute of Chicago. During her tenure there from 1942 to 1959 she expanded the museum's collection with a wide range of the best examples of contemporary work.

A savvy and resourceful woman, Katharine Kuh offered her expertise to numerous Chicago collectors in exchange for, say, a Mondrian or a Matisse. "I'd travel with them or meet them in Paris, and in return for advising them about their own collections, pick out paintings for the museum within a certain price range. I think when I came we had about two paintings by Picasso. I think when I left we had maybe seventeen or nineteen."

I'm not so keen about growing old. Eighty-seven isn't the best of ages. The problem is that my mind constantly outstrips my body. My body is not worth two cents. In fact, if I could just take the whole darn thing, toss it out the window, and just keep my mind and eyes, I think I'd be very happy. [Laughs.] But the fact that I have to live with this exhausted, worn-out, old rag of a mechanism is very difficult, and frustrating . . . very frustrating.

I've never liked the way I looked, but now I even go so far as to avoid looking at myself in the mirror; I avoid looking. Oh, I think I look terrible. At eighty-seven you're not going to be Greta Garbo. But even Greta Garbo (I used to see her walking up and down Madison Avenue years ago, you know) began to look pretty wrinkled when she got older. Her eyes were still piercing, but I'm sure she wouldn't have talked to you about the pleasures of old age. [Laughs.]

All my life I've been ill off and on, so I'm well prepared for this stage. From the age of ten to twenty-one I wore a plaster cast because I had polio. I remember one time I went to a doctor in Boston. I was sitting in this doctor's office and there was a man sitting in a wheelchair, and that man was Franklin Roosevelt. He was going to the same doctor that I went to because he was also paralyzed. I was about fifteen, and he hadn't become president yet, but he'd been working in government, and I recognized him from his pictures because anyone who had polio could see that he had it. He was attended by an Afro-American, who was kind of like a valet, and he sent him out on an errand. We were waiting there, just the two of us, in the waiting room. He was reading the newspaper, and he dropped it, and he looked to me because he couldn't pick it up; he had big leg braces and everything. So he asked me if I could pick it up for him, and I was so embarrassed because at fifteen you didn't like to admit that you were wearing a plaster cast. I said, "Well, I can't stoop because I'm in a plaster cast." And he was charming. He said, "Well, with my legs and your plaster cast we make a good team."

I've often wondered whether Roosevelt ever would have become president of this country if he hadn't been paralyzed. I think if you'll examine people who have had polio, you'll find that they are so challenged by that darned disease that they do all kinds of things. Having been somewhat paralyzed, always having more pain than the other fella, made me a better person. Because I was a bit lame and crooked when I was younger I always knew that I would have to fight to get what I wanted. If I hadn't had polio, I might not have had as interesting a life. The funny thing is, my polio is returning now. I have a thing called post-polio syndrome. All the muscles that took over are now exhausted. They're all absolutely gone. So I'm more paralyzed now than I was before and in more pain; it's like living through it a second time.

This time it just gets progressively more painful. But otherwise everything goes fine. It's just hard to go to an exhibition because I can't stand up for any length of time.

It frustrates me, sure, but somehow or other I still enjoy my life, I really do. I'm telling you the truth. I enjoy it, because I could end it if I wanted to. I don't consider that such a terrible thing to do. I think perhaps before we fall apart too completely it would be a rather generous thing to do. But I'm not ready yet, obviously, or I would have done it. I'm still too involved with life, with art, with people. I'm still doing a certain amount of writing, I'm still doing advisory work, I'm still seeing young and interesting artists. No, my life is still full, and I'm grateful, grateful. So if I had to choose between having my mind or having my body, I would choose my mind.

One nice thing about being eighty-seven is that I don't have to worry at all about the future, because I know pretty much it's going to be downhill from here on. So I really take each hour for the pleasure it brings. If it doesn't bring pleasure, then I figure the next hour will, and generally it does. I'm not in the least bit terrified of dying, and it's not because I'm religious, but rather because I'm not. You see, I think your life is your only gift. So all my life I've been driven to extract the most from it—to grab it, enjoy it, use it. And I think I have used it for enrichment. Now that my body is giving out, death is much less unpleasant to consider. I've lived a good life, so I'm much less afraid of dying.

My one great fear is getting a stroke and being left

completely without control. I've left a living will with very strong statements about no intravenous feeding and no tubes. I have a very dear friend in Chicago who is a year or two older than I am, and she's just had a couple of strokes and she's blanked out. I understand they're feeding her. Now that, I think, is wrong. She can't get better. What's the good? She had a wonderful, productive, creative life. Isn't that enough?

I've really reached the stage where I say to myself, "Oh, you don't have to do one thing you don't want. You don't have to prove anything anymore. You don't have to succeed or fail or anything. Whatever you do now is just to enrich other people and yourself if you can." That about sums up my philosophy of aging.

Maggie Kuhn

❯ ❯ ❯ ❯ ❯ ❯ ❯ ❯ ❯

*When Maggie Kuhn and five of her friends found themselves
in mandatory retirement at sixty-five they were enraged. So
enraged, in fact, that they decided to form the Gray Panthers. What began as a radical protest group in the early
1970s has now grown into an international multigenera-
tional organization.*

*In many ways Maggie Kuhn has been rewarded for her
dedication to her beliefs. The 1978* World Almanac *named
her one of the twenty-five most influential women in America. The* Ladies Home Journal *honored her as one of*

125

America's 100 most important women. But in spite of the accolades, Maggie's self-image and daily routine remain unchanged. "I've always had demanding jobs and have worked hard, but I'm working harder today than I ever did. That's a delight and a satisfaction. The fact that I can do it, despite infirmities, delights me. And also the fact that there is a growing readiness to view old age as a triumph, not a disaster." She is eighty-six, and recently published her memoir No Stone Unturned: The Life and Times of Maggie Kuhn.

The Gray Panthers have reached many old people; we have about 70,000 in our networks. Many of them have come out of social change organizations, out of the peace movement, out of the labor movement, out of social work. These are people who are concerned about their neighbor, concerned about social justice issues. And these people are not going to stop because they're retired or old. There's a new kind of energy that comes from late life, a new freedom. Unfortunately, few in our society understand that. Ours is a youth-oriented country, no doubt about it.

We have been monitoring commercial television—and radio to some degree—for more than a decade. By and large, age has been denied, glossed over. It doesn't exist. There's a fear of old people in this country. Gerontophobia is an epidemic; the fear of old people and the fear of growing old, the two are combined. It goes back, I think, to the fact that we've made a fetish of being young. We pride ourselves on being a youthful nation, and yet a growing percentage of our population has achieved a great old age. I think it goes back to our economic system too, because we worship the bottom line—productivity, the almighty dollar. In our society you're deemed old when you can't work, they don't want you to work, or you don't want to work. Old age is just anathema in our youth-centered, capitalistic, acquisitive, private-centered society. In America, it is a bad scene to be old.

The isolation of old people in this country and the segregation of old people is deadly, deadly. We old folks need to be the mentors of the young. The young need us just as much as we need them. The possibility of finding the commonalities between the old and the young excites me. I'd like to declare a moratorium on retirement communities; let's not build any more. Let's share our space, the young and the old together. The cost of living in a retirement home is extraordinary, so why not stay where you are and share your space with young people?

Six years ago I helped to organize the Shared Housing Resource Center, which has done extraordinarily well. We are in touch with some 400 communities across the country where there are different kinds of shared housing. In Philadelphia during the past two years we've successfully matched 300 people. We persuade some old person who lives alone (you know, kicking and screaming!) to share his or her home with a young person, like a student or something—and there are some wonderful exchanges. I have all kinds of stuff—

dishes, linens, furniture—and young people just have books and sleeping bags and stereos, but no stuff! [Laughs.] So we exchange.

It's a viable human solution. People hate to leave their homes. Many people die shortly after they have left; it's a traumatic thing that some never recover from. If there is the option of staying where you've lived, in neighborhoods that you know, what a joy that is and what security. The opportunity to tell your stories and your jokes and sing your songs and share your books with young people is an absolute delight. But there has to be a willingness to share. And we oldsters have a lot to share.

You know, when people say to me that I am "eighty-six years young," I'm a bit offended. Because to say that I'm eighty-six years young is to deny my history and all the things that I've done and all the changes that I've seen. I'm convinced that it's harder to be young than old. The young are not sure of a future. I am having—and I say this quite candidly and gratefully—a glorious old age. Sure, I have arthritis; I have very severe arthritis in my hands. It's very hard for me to open things and turn off a light switch; there are lots of things I cannot do. I have arthritis in my knees too, and at times it's very painful and I have difficulty walking. But there's nothing wrong with my head, thank goodness, and nothing wrong with my spirit. I've discovered the marvelous gift of compensation in old age. When people lose the feeling in one part of their body or one of their senses they adapt and develop a willingness and an ability to survive and thrive.

I believe that there has to be a purpose and a goal to life. The secret of thriving and surviving is having a goal. Having a goal is absolutely essential, because it gives you the energy and the drive to do what you must do, and to get up when you feel like staying in bed.

I have plenty of goals! On my eightieth birthday, in fact, I vowed to myself that I would do something outrageous at least once a week, and for the past few years I've been able to live up to that promise. On a more practical note, I've got daily chores to do. I have to get up early to feed the cats. And I like to take a morning bubble bath. I like to soak in the tub—right up to my neck, you know, just soak—and do a little exercising in the tub. It keeps that pain under control, and it limbers and comforts. Then I'm ready to start my day. I come down and have breakfast. I like to eat breakfast and look at the paper and play with the cats and think about what's ahead for the day and do some immediate planning. And every day, every day is some surprise. I look for that. What's going to be new, what's new today? There is seldom a day without some element of surprise. I think in a sense surprise is synonymous with hope.

One of the lovely things in my life was that one time I had a young lover. He was forty years younger than I. We had lots in common and he told me that I helped him through some very painful, late adolescence growing pains. In so-called primitive societies, the older women are the ones who introduce the young men, at puberty, to their sexual roles. And older women can be great lovers.

So I believe that we can't, in late life, get set in our ways—fixed on what we used to do, on what was accustomed, or on what others expect us to do. We must always be open to each new day, to the future. My ability to survive and keep on plugging is an outgrowth of my passion for hope and change. I'm often asked about burnout, but I haven't burned out. I've been working intensively, you know, since 1970. That's a long time. My recipe is that if something doesn't work out, you back away from it and try something new. Again, you're always open to an emerging issue, an emerging trend, a new idea. Creativity and the joy of creativity are reinforced by new ideas. We must always be open to each new day, to the future, to new opportunities. They're there, but we have to be ready to see them.

Stanley Kunitz

❧   ❧   ❧   ❧   ❧   ❧   ❧   ❧   ❧

I used to fantasize a great deal about what would happen to me in my old age. The fantasy that stayed with
me was that in my old age I would be a gardener on a
great estate and I would have a little lodge and solitude
and I would work on the earth. Of course, I've been a
passionate gardener all my life, so this would have been
a very good solution for my problems. And that's probably what would have happened had I not managed to
survive as a writer.

Stanley Kunitz is considered our senior statesman of poetry. His hard-earned literary reputation is now secure and un-questioned. Those familiar with his poetry accord him high praise. He's tough in the sense of being a survivor of tough times, wistful, serene, and proud of having lived a life in service of art. In conversation he is eloquent and intense, yet never without a twinkle in his eye. We talked in his book-lined New York apartment, a place abundant with greenery and sprinkled with antique treasures acquired for modest sums a half century ago. That's the external world of Stanley Kunitz. His internal world, despite his eighty-six years, continues to be the world of poetry. Being an older artist has not diminished his excitement for his work; his desire to write is as intense and immediate as when he was young.

I'm really too busy to think about being old. There's still so much work yet to be done. I'm as curious as I ever was. I can't wait for the day to begin and get going. An artist is never retired. The excitements, the obligations, the adventure—all that is just as alive for me now as it was when I was much younger. I don't feel any diminu-tion of energy, and actually my physical energy is almost as good as it ever was. I can work harder and drink longer and stay awake longer than most of my young friends. The only noticeable change is that I had to give up tennis a few years ago because of an arthritic condi-tion. But I still work long hours in my garden, I still walk long distances. And I need to, because I don't like to be tied to my desk. The only real deficiency of the writing vocation is that it's too sedentary.

I think it takes tremendous courage to live well, and that holds true at any age in life. The courage comes out of knowing that if you don't persist, you fail. The courage to be is the courage to dare. To dare to explore all one's guilts, one's shames, one's defeats, everything that has happened to you—that is all part of life, and beautiful if you can turn it into art. Nothing is alien to art, nothing is forbidden, nothing is impossible, as long as you create the form, as long as you create something whole and something true. That's what I aspire to do.

In one's early years, one writes out of one's glands— really out of the juices of the libido—and everything seems absolutely marvelous and right and easy. But in one's early years you don't know enough, you're not wise enough, to say important things; you're merely reacting to experience. In late life you have wisdom to draw from.

I've never stopped being excited about my art. Every new poem is equally exciting to me and also equally impossible. I never feel that it is going to be easy, that I can sit down at my desk and toss off a poem. I have to dig for it and in fact the more I know about this craft, this art, this vocation, the more difficult it is to say what I want to say. But maybe that's just because my standards are higher these days because I expect more from the art. The next poem always seems impossible.

The beautiful thing about the poem before it is written is that it's perfect. We are mortal and fallible human beings, and we have our limitations. And the poem that is written is never as good as the poem I imagine I am going to write. My thought about being a poet is that, especially in this society, one has chosen not to be a success. There's no way of being a success as a poet that's comparable to being the head of General Motors or living in the White House. Success in poetry is almost a secret to the mass of the population. So one ought not to delude oneself that a degree of recognition involves being a success. The only success that ought to mean anything is in terms of one's appraisal of oneself. Have I done as much as I could have done? Have I really fulfilled all my expectations? And, of course, I haven't. I'm constantly in a state of discontent. So, as far as I'm concerned, I'm not a success and I never will be, and I don't want to be.

My life has been full of setbacks and disappointments. I free-lanced for almost twenty years because I wasn't able to sell my poetry and nobody wanted me to teach it. I scrabbled for a living almost constantly. I lived on a farm and I worked that farm daily. And my feeling's always been that the natural world not only was a means for survival for me, it gave me something I could trust. It could never betray me because it responded to my ministrations and it was beautiful. I loved and still love the sense of growing the marvelous returns of one's labors and the beauty of what grows. To me it's so thrilling that I can hardly wait to see each morning what happens during the night. In those lonely years of solitude I sank into myself in an attempt to salvage what I could of what seemed a rather desperate existence. As it turned out, it was unhappy for me in terms of my marriage—my first marriage—so that when I think of black times I think of those years. Yet they were beautiful years too, and to me they are entwined like different colored threads.

I suppose if you live as I have you are bound to have encountered along the way many disappointments: early disappointments in love, disappointments in your work, failure in expectations—there are so many of them I could hardly count them. The death of friends, people you love; it's a history of losses, much of it. And it reinforces your essential tragic sense. I suppose my basic view of experience is that our life is tragic and yet it is full of comedy, and the very fact that you take yourself so seriously is one of its comic aspects. Measured against the whole cosmos none of us is important. I don't think it is possible to build a full and creative life out of anger or frustration or resentment. These are all destructive elements and in the end they will destroy you and destroy your art. The only basis for art is affection. You have to begin by liking yourself and you have to like others more. If you don't have that feeling of living in an affectionate universe, I think you'll perish, simply out of bile and bitterness.

In a curious way I think that with age comes a diminishing of barriers. You can take greater risks at a certain point because you don't care anymore. You've tested yourself, you know what you can do, you know better than anyone else and who's to stop you from daring to do something that is not expected from you?

It's funny, but death always seemed to me more frightful when I was twenty than it does now. It paralyzed me more at that age. And the reason is that now you know you've done what you could, done it as well as you could, and there's a sense of maturation, a sense, to a degree, of fulfillment. Not that one is ever completely fulfilled. But to a degree at least, to a degree you've done what you expected of yourself. You've learned through the cycles of nature, through the seasons, and the stars, the tides, that there's a time for everything, and there's a time to go too. And as you age there is perhaps a greater acceptance of this whole phenomenon of dying as well as of living. And then there's that other aspect that in your age, death itself becomes implicit in your voice. It becomes your theme in an intimate way, just as sexual love, let's say, became your intimate theme in your twenties. So you're exploring new territory and there's that close embrace between your life and your death that you never had before. That does something to your poetry—inevitably it has to. This poem I wrote recently, just after the death of a friend—a neighbor on Cape Cod—is called "The Long Boat":

> When his boat snapped loose
> from its moorings, under
> the screaking of the gulls,
> he tried at first to wave
> to his dear ones on shore,
> but in the rolling fog
> they had already lost their faces.
> Too tired even to choose
> between jumping and calling,
> somehow he felt absolved and free
> of his burdens, those mottoes

stamped on his name-tag:
conscience, ambition and all
that caring.
He was content to lie down
with the family ghosts
in the slop of his cradle,
buffeted by the storm,
endlessly drifting.
Peace, Peace!
To be rocked by the Infinite
As if it didn't matter
which way was home;
as if it didn't know
he loved the earth so much
he wanted to stay forever.

Above all what I feel right now is a beautiful richness of life, how lucky I was to be born. Just think: if I hadn't been born, I'd never have been able to share with you this moment, ever experienced not only the joys, but the griefs. Even though things sometimes went wrong, terribly wrong, looking back on life I feel great joy about being alive. Of all the gifts that one could imagine, I cannot think of a greater one than life itself.

Frances Lear

≫   ≫   ≫   ≫   ≫   ≫   ≫   ≫   ≫

In 1985, at the age of sixty-two, Frances Lear was divorced from her husband, the television producer Norman Lear. Within a year she created Lear's, *a glossy fashion magazine geared to the forty-plus woman. Smart, classy, and brassy, Frances Lear has been a tireless crusader for older women.*

T he major thing about growing older is that my body seems to be fighting my mind. My body gets worse, my mind gets better. And the older I get, the more this basic conflict grows in severity. Now, don't get me wrong; I'm extraordinarily satisfied and happy to be the age that I am—which is sixty-seven—but I wish I had my old body back.

When I began to lose my looks, I went to pieces. I thought, "This is the end of life and I have nothing left." So I had my face lifted. I have always cared a lot about clothes and makeup and hair and how I looked. As an attractive woman, I always tried to be even more attractive. I worked at it. I think the problem with this whole area in women's lives is that they don't work hard enough to be attractive, that they don't dress correctly. I mean, we all have a look that's becoming to us, so we should darn well keep that look on us every day. We should do something about our makeup, we should do something about our hair, and we should have plastic surgery. My heavens, I can't imagine not having plastic surgery if you can afford it.

In addition to staying attractive, I also think you have to be much more charming, much wittier, much more interesting the older you get. I can sit next to a man who has on his other side a gorgeous twenty-five-year-old, and he'll talk to me, because I'm much more interesting. I ask him questions about himself: "What do you do? How much money do you make? What do you do with your money?" and so on. It's such fun, it's such a challenge.

It seems to me that I have, as an impetus to stay young looking, a strong interest in sex. Men, on the other hand, seem less and less interested in sex the older they get. They are afraid that they're going to lose their virility, that they will not be able to have sex, and so on. But I deal with it in a very strong, positive way. The more I attract men, and the more active I am sexually, the younger I am.

I have a theory that we exist only as we compare ourselves to externals. For example, I have no self-esteem unless I compare myself to you, because my self-esteem cannot be measured unless it can be measured against something else. What I have come to understand is that it is not in my mind that I'm going to make a difference; the difference is going to come from what I do on the outside. If I produce a successful magazine, for example, people will start to think of me as a woman who is talented and capable. So self-esteem, self-confidence, comes from getting up off your ass and going out and earning it.

You know, I don't remember having an extended time—ever—of being happy when I was younger than sixty. My life changed dramatically, totally, profoundly, when I was sixty. I remember quite vividly when I turned sixty. I said to myself, This is the moment when one starts looking ahead and counting. Up until that time I never looked ahead. I had said, This is my life and it started when I was born, and that's all I could see. Now I see the time ahead of me and what I would like to accomplish in that time. I think that's why I have become more focused. I realized that I really didn't have much time to waste.

The most important experience in my life has been to find a purpose for it. I always have to have a mission, although the mission changes. When I was a child it was to support the labor movement, which has gone quite a distance since then. I will find, I'm sure, another mission after my present one, but right now I'm trying to make women who are not young more attractive—both to industry and to themselves. My personal satisfaction comes from being recognized as someone who has achieved something, someone who has influenced our culture. I love to influence. I want to take the next issue and influence that issue. I also want to be happy, I want to have a good time, I want to laugh, I want to love, but I want most of all to influence.

I have no religion other than a deep belief in the value of personal freedom. I believe in heroism. I believe in prevailing over odds. What makes it possible for me and for other older women to stand tall? Our wills, nothing else. If you don't want it bad enough, you're not going to stand tall. You have to care so much that you are willing to suffer for it. We suffered in the women's movement. There were bodies strewn on the beaches that will never stand up, but look what we got. And unless we keep fighting, unless there is passion in us, unless there's movement, unless there is surprise, achievement, all of these things, we die young. We must exercise the muscle in our head in order to live a long and productive and terrific life. And whatever in you is negative or dark, fight it, get it out, put the light on it, and turn it around and make it positive.

George Leonard

⯈ ⯈ ⯈ ⯈ ⯈ ⯈ ⯈ ⯈ ⯈

I tend not to think about the fact that I'm getting older until people bring it to my attention. I'm sixty-seven, but I really don't feel that old. The truth of the matter is I feel just the same. One of my mentors was Dan Mish, the editor-in-chief of *Look*. Someone said he had the appearance of a Renaissance archbishop and wielded approximately the same power. Anyway, I was over at his house and after a few drinks I said, "You know, Dan, you just turned sixty." He said, "When you get up here it feels just the same. It's just the same." You know, when you're young you look at an old person and say, "Well, it must be very different." But it's not different; it's just the same. You see a good-looking woman, you have that same feeling. You see a football game, you ask yourself, Why couldn't I run out and catch that pass? I still do a lot of exercise, I still play a crazy game of frisbee, and I practice aikido daily. I know intellectually that I'm aging, but it doesn't feel that different. Everything seems about the same.

George Leonard is the author of many books, including Education and Ecstasy, The Ultimate Athlete, *and, most recently,* Mastery. *He served as senior editor of* Look *magazine from 1953 to 1970, where he earned many national awards. He is currently a contributing editor for* Esquire. *A devoted athlete, he holds a third-degree black belt in the martial art of aikido and is the co-owner of an aikido school in Mill Valley, California, where he makes his home.*

When I was twenty or so back in the 1940s I was interested in swing music. I had a thirteen-piece swing band, and we played Benny Goodman and Count Basie arrangements, and it was the biggest thrill in my life. I never achieved that kind of glory since and I never will again—to have a very successful big band and play at all the dances in your hometown, and even tour. But I was absolutely unathletic. I was a skinny kid, you know. And at that time skinny was considered disgraceful. In the

1930s, muscle tone wasn't even considered. Look back at old *Life* magazines—they have all these beefcake pictures of lifeguards, and all of them were fat—so I really was kind of an outsider. I never got into sports until in my forties. I'm one of those late-blooming jocks. I started aikido at age forty-seven, then got into the running craze when I was fifty. If I'd been running at twenty, God knows how fast I'd be running now, but I wasn't running at twenty. So the truth of the matter is that I could run faster at age fifty than I could at age twenty.

Just yesterday I was with a group of aging people, and we were with a young exercise physiologist who had created an exercise program for us. One of the things she had us do was hit a ball against a wall. She said, "This is very important, because as we get older we lose our hand-eye coordination." I was about to say something, but I kept my mouth shut. So then she has us jump up and down for a while and stand on one foot for ten seconds. "This is important," she said, "because as we grow older our sense of balance begins to fall off." And I said, "Wait, hold it, hold it. Our sense of balance might fall off. Our hand-eye coordination might fall off. But they might also improve." She was all flustered. I said, "Don't do us any more favors. This is ageism, and I will fight it on every front." So I said, "Okay, let's do some coordination things. How old are you?" "Twenty," she says. "I'm sixty-seven," I said, "and my reflex is obviously much slower than yours. Obviously my synoptic connections are not going to be as good as yours." I'm getting her kind of scared, you know? Then I said, "Let's do this game." And I got her doing this hand-slapping reaction game, and she couldn't even touch me. We also played this little game of pushing each other off balance. I was clobbering her all over the place.

The point I went on to make to this young woman is this: If at age twenty I was operating at 80 percent of my potential, and then at age sixty I was operating at 80 percent of my potential, obviously the twenty-year-old would win. But how many of us are working at 80 percent of our potential at age twenty? Very few—a tiny, tiny percentage. So the possibility exists that if I start training myself at age forty-seven in aikido, and now, at sixty-seven, I'm operating at 80 percent of my potential, in balance and coordination I'm a lot better than I was at age twenty when I only operated at 10 percent of my potential. When you see things in this light, you can improve at any age.

Unlike so many people, I don't see the spiritual as disconnected from the body. One of the great mistakes of the great religious traditions is that all of them have denigrated the body as being mere flesh, all evil, a gift of Satan. Our job is to get as far away as possible from the body to achieve enlightenment. I think that's a mistake. Modern physics shows us that matter is just another form of energy—a very compacted, relatively stable form of energy. So one of the most encouraging things for me has been the growth of the participatory sports movement in the United States. I think we must change our attitude toward the body, and our attitude toward aging. Like my wife now; she achieved a black belt in aikido, but as a kid she lay around and read books, literature and philosophy. She never ran at all. Now she says, "Come on out, show me how to catch a ball so we can play better." We have gloves and bats and softballs, all sorts of sports equipment. And she does aerobics and her coordination's gotten much better. At first she couldn't throw a frisbee, but now she really whips it out there. She's a much better athlete now than she was at age twenty, much better. Of course, as you get older you sometimes run into arthritis, things like that, and then you're necessarily limited. But whatever the limits are you can always do a little more than you think you can, and you can get a certain pleasure out of that. I think a big part of the whole aging story is staying in shape.

I challenge you to watch television commercials for a week. Approximately half the commercials show a climactic moment. You see beautiful, incredibly slim young people—sometimes they've already run the race—jumping up and down and throwing frosty cans of diet cola or beer to each other. It's a climactic moment. You see men working for one and a half seconds, and then it's Miller time. Television has become the chief value giver of this age. In previous times it was the tribal elder, the village elder, perhaps the family, the extended family, but those agents have all withered away. The media have stepped in to take their place.

Television commercials are specifically about value. What they're telling you is what to value—and you buy what you value. Money is a pretty damn direct feedback mechanism to see what we value. Now, the underlying rhythm that the commercials point out as the ideal rhythm of our culture is a series of climactic moments moving up, up, up, another climax, another climax, and you level off and then you go right back up again, right back up again. Quick weight loss diets, credit card spending, get it quick. There is no long curve at all, there's no plateau at all. And what does this mean if you are an older person in America, a person who has achieved any wisdom at all? Well, purely and simply, it takes you out of the loop. Unless you have the energy and stamina to have one climactic moment after the next, you're doomed, aren't you? This quick-fix mentality, more than anything else, knocks old people out, because you've got to be on the way up—the yuppie, you know. You've got an MBA from Harvard and you get that seventy thousand dollar job—your wife does too—and you buy a condo in Manhattan and you're on your way. And you've got to keep consuming, you've got to get a yacht, you've got to go on a wine and castle tour to southern France, and you've got to come back to your dinner parties and talk about it. It's a little harder for old people to do that, so the quick-fix mentality cuts them out of the picture.

I've had a chance to look at aging in America because my mother lives in a retirement community. I see that people who didn't have many resources, who were not very interested in life when they were younger, become miserable rather quickly. I've noticed that as you get older you desperately need other people, friends and so forth. If you're preoccupied with yourself, you've had it—the whole universe will become yourself. The universe will become your pains and aches and your complaints, and when the universe becomes your complaint, then it's not a very nice place to live in.

I think it's important to stay interested, to stay vitally interested in world affairs; to have some religious interest is very important; to have interest in other people; to have a community of people with whom you really share things, not superficially, but with whom you share your worries as well as your triumphs. I see the possibility of having a very good old age.

I suppose it's all a matter of desire. I certainly would like to recommend things that involve the body, if possible—some of the old favorites like yoga, t'ai chi, things that have a meditative aspect in them, because then you do tend to get the spiritual. And the spiritual is simply turning off the chatter. I'm not particularly interested in what god or what religion you follow, so long as you can get that focus or concentration and leave off the eternal chatter of daily life. Then the world rolls right into you, the world and all of its glory rolls right into you—and that's the wonder of existence.

Eda LeShan

> > > > > > > >

Eda LeShan is a noted educator, family counselor, and author of over twenty books, including When Your Child Drives You Crazy, The Wonderful Crisis of Middle Age, *and, most recently,* It's Better to Be Over the Hill Than Under It: Thoughts on Life Over Sixty. *She is a contributing editor of* Woman's Day, *for which she writes a monthly column, "Talking It Over." For three years she was moderator of the Emmy-nominated public television series "How Do Your Children Grow?" She lives in New York with her husband, Lawrence LeShan.*

W hile working on a book I was writing on middle age I was asked by an oceanographer if I knew anything about lobsters. "Lobsters? I'm sorry, but it really has never been very high on my list of priorities to wonder about that." And he said, "Well, I'm going to explain it to you. Did you know that lobsters know when they have to deshell? They get real crowded inside this three-pound shell—they're terribly uncomfortable—and it's not possible for them to go on living if they stay in that shell. So what they do is go out to the sea unprotected, which is very dangerous—they might get hit by a reef, they might be eaten by another lobster or a fish—but they must deshell. That whole, hard shell comes off and the pink membrane that's inside grows and becomes a harder shell, but a bigger one."

At first it didn't hit me, but soon I became preoccupied with lobsters. I kept coming back to the idea and I thought, That's the most interesting thing. I dreamed about it. Finally, I mentioned it to my therapist and she said, "Eda, that's what you're writing this book on middle age about. Going to the reef, even if it's dangerous." And that really has been my philosophy of life, at any age, and it certainly is now. You know, if you stay stifled where you are, you're dead before you're dead. So the thing you need more than anything else when you get old is the courage of the lobster. You are going to go through things where you have to become much more flexible. You have to be willing to change, you have to face painful crisis, and courage is absolutely the most essential part of it. Courage and a sense of humor, that's what you need.

But I have to tell you, I'm not all that optimistic that a great many older people will find the courage in their lives to make them better. My observation of older people is that they simply become more of what they've always been. If they've had the capacity for self-acceptance, for courage, for the enjoyment of being alone, and for the enjoyment of nature and so forth, then it's going to be more so as they get older. Whereas the crotchety, bitter, depressed people only get worse. "Why haven't you made my life happier?" is their most common complaint. I have one friend who asked his wife to make a list of what it would take to make her happy, and every single thing depended on him. And I think there are a hell of a lot of older women who are like that and who have a deep sense of dissatisfaction, especially in our generation. They didn't do the kinds of things they wanted to do when they were younger because they didn't have a chance to pursue the profession of their dreams. You know, their brothers went to medical and law school and they were told to stay home until they got married. There's a lot of bitterness, and I don't think that they're going to overcome it. Some will, of course, and that's the hope, but most will not. Who's going to help them see they have the choice? That's the thing I think you have to look at. That's where support groups and experts and counselors are just as much needed for older people as for children or younger people. But I think it's pretty tough for a lot of

154 · Eda LeShan

people to change that much as they get older. There's
a kind of rigidity that sets in, and it's hard to break
through it. On the other hand, I can say that I get the
most fantastic mail from people who do understand,
people who are changing for the better, and it is terribly
gratifying.

Meditation is very important for older people, not
only because it gives you this kind of enrichment of your
inner life, but because it also puts you into a phase in
which you begin to be ready for dying, which is to be
part of the universe and to give up the material sense of
being. I think it would be wonderful if retirement homes
had meditation programs instead of pinochle games. Oh,
they could have pinochle games too, but it shouldn't all
be focused on activity. And I think right now it mostly
is.

It is important to have rich inner resources, but most
seniors don't work at it. If you have spent your whole
life in outward relationships, if material things have
dominated your environment—if that's been your
focus—I think it's very hard to get inner richness because you haven't worked on it. There's so much emphasis these days for middle-aged and younger people to
develop self-awareness and touching and meditation
techniques, but no emphasis for seniors to do the same.
And that's unfortunate, because the child within may
not have been let out of the bag since she was four—
she's sleeping, you know. I really believe that older
people who see that they have a choice can change, but
they have to see it first.

Inner life is really about play. And for those who have

kept the sense of the child in themselves alive, that's
where it comes out—it comes out in meditation, in
nature walks, and so on. If I take a walk and I see
beautiful leaves or I pick up an acorn or I watch people
or I feed ducks, those are childlike, playful things, but
they have to do with an inner life. A lot of people
haven't got that. The denial of aging in our culture is
related to that. Value has not been placed on the inner
life; it's been on outer productivity. So when people get
older and they're in rest homes, or they sit a long time
and look at the ocean, or they wait for the sunset and
then they wait after the sunset for the stars, there's a lot
of time in there where they might be doing "nothing."
We think of it as wasting time. There is a sense of having
to be busy all the time, and I'm afraid that is a big part
of the culture.

We are really afraid to be alone in our culture. I
didn't ever understand or appreciate solitude until
maybe twenty or thirty years ago as I got middle-aged.
It happened on Long Beach Island off the coast of New
Jersey, where I had gone for a small vacation. I went in
April and it was practically deserted and there was a
terrible fog over everything. The foghorns were blaring
and there was a lighthouse you could hardly see and I
rented a cottage. For the first three days I had a nervous
breakdown. I cried, I ate too much, I couldn't stand it.
About the third day I looked out and the sun had come
out and there was this wonderful lighthouse and dunes,
and the little sandpipers were walking along, and I went
out for a walk and I met some fisherman and I waded out
to an old wreck, and all of a sudden it dawned on

me—all of a sudden I realized there's only one companion I've got from birth to death and that's me, and by God I can have a good time with myself. I brought along some clay, and I did some sculptures while I was there. I stayed for about a week or ten days. That was a real turning point in my life.

I later found that being away in the country provided me with one of my favorite forms of meditation, feeding ducks. When we lived in Cape Cod for ten years there was a lake and I had about thirty ducks who came to me every day and became my friends—they even walked into the house if the door was open. As I got older, nature became alive, the universe and everything in it. I came to agree with my husband Larry's theory that as you get older there's an unconscious moving toward the spiritual, a desire to be part of the universe as a whole, and that it is a kind of preparation for death. It's about moving beyond a state of denial toward a deeper and deeper sense of appreciation of life itself.

I believe that courage implies a lack of denial, that you really are willing to face the issues, whatever they are, and that you grow from them; that there's nothing that happens to you as long as you're alive that you don't learn from. Since I just had a stroke, I will be learning about strokes for the next year or two. I certainly have already developed a much more profound sense of how important my life is and how precious life is. People live through terrible things—widowhood and suffering and pain and operations and all these things—and every damn one of them teaches you something if you use it. This has been true of our marriage. For forty-seven years we've gone through one crisis after another, but there wasn't a single one that we didn't grow and learn from and become much stronger. And I think that's been the basis of our life. Somebody once asked my daughter what it felt like to be the child of two psychologists and her answer was, "They made all the mistakes that everybody else makes, but I knew they were trying to grow and change." I think that's about it.

Bella Lewitzky

⯈   ⯈   ⯈   ⯈   ⯈   ⯈   ⯈   ⯈   ⯈

I must confess that, except for the nagging little physical things, I find this age absolutely treasurable. I love being my age. How old am I? I'm seventy-four. No, seventy-five. Oh, I'm not quite sure. Who cares! [Laughs.]

Bella Lewitzky has had a long and productive career as a dancer, choreographer, and teacher. In 1966 she established the Lewitzky Dance Company in Los Angeles. The twelve-

member troupe has drawn rave reviews for their inventive explorations of space, drama, and ritual.

I think there are a lot of pluses to growing old. I find, for example, that the years I have lived have taught me to look at things differently than a very young person. A young person says, "It's a disaster, I'm going to kill myself, nothing good is going to come of this," but I say, "I've been there before, honey, it will wear out, you will survive, relax." So the wonderful essence of having lived this long is that you can look forward with the past as a reference. That is an attribute you can only purchase by living. You need experiences. You need to know what it is like to have had multiple emotional experiences, acquired stories, watched your friends and other people's lives, had a child, and undergone major things that would affect one's life. Those happen as your actual physical prowess is declining—so they happen at opposite rates—but they substitute for one another quite beautifully. You see, I'm a collector. It's the collection of incidents—rather than single revelatory incidents—that make up the whole for me and which have made me, I hope, wiser.

I'm a very optimistic person. I'm one of those people who will join any organization. One part of my mind says, Bella, you know that this probably will fail. Why are you joining it? But another part of my mind says, It may make things better, let's join it. And that side usually wins. Indeed, I feel that there is always a tomorrow and always another adventure. I have a mind of tremendous curiosity. I feel I haven't learned nearly enough, and I just hope there will be many more years left to continue learning.

I feel very fortunate that I'm in a profession where retirement is not a meaningful word. Artists do not retire because most artists do not have a job; they have a view of life which they practice and they continue that practice until they no longer draw breath. I've never wanted to be otherwise employed. If I fire myself, it will have to be for a very good reason, but I don't see that in the immediate future.

I suppose I'm always looking to the future, leaving the past to the past, because it's enervating to worry about something you cannot change. Beyond learning from it, focusing on the past seems a waste of energy, a waste of time. It is no fun—and the things that I do are fun. I love looking at what the next day holds—most of the time. Sometimes I'm a bit alarmed at the society we have made; injustice has always troubled me, and there is a lot of it out there.

It's funny, but as I've aged I've grown more confident in my own values yet, at the same time, more tolerant of differences. I probably was a very intolerant young person. After all, most teenagers know exactly what is wrong with the world and how to correct it. All teenagers are invincible and all-knowing, and so by the time I hit middle-adulthood I was an intolerant scientific humanist. But as I have grown older I have said, "Let's look at all of the ways and make a judgment." Today I profoundly believe that you cannot look only at the past,

and you cannot look only at the future. The past becomes a ground of relativity to help you judge the
present; the future becomes a dream whereby you pit
the present to climb toward another phase of the present. But they are interrelated growth processes.

I do so hope the future years will bring something
unexpected. I love surprising things that happen to me
and they always have, so I hope I always remain open to
such invitations. This is my life attitude and it has no age
definition. The dream of the future is not relegated to
youth, but is an ongoing process in life. Youth does not
have the ability to look back, and that, I guess, is why
elders are revered in certain societies. Elders have the
ability to say, ''I have seen that; it happens this way; you
might consider that.''

I was very pleasantly surprised, oh, about ten years
ago, when I was part of a cultural committee that went
to China. On this committee I was seated first, was
given all kinds of special courtesies, and listened to a
little bit more than other people. It was very funny for
me, and I kept asking myself, Why on earth is this
happening to me here? And then suddenly I went, Oh,
but of course, they worship the elderly. This is their
Confucius dialogue; they feel that the elders need to be
honored. And I was the oldest—decidedly the oldest—
member of that committee. So instead of relishing the
fact that maybe I was wiser, I had to concede I was the
oldest. It was fun to come from a society like ours where
elders are like tissue paper, thrown away, and go into a
society where elders are revered and held in high regard.
I'm not sure that's always as it should be, but I do know

from the life I've lived that there are times when you really do need to listen to somebody who's been there before you and then be able to discard what they say if you don't believe in it. At least they've been there. As for me, life continues to be a "work in progress," and I plan to continue working.

Art Linkletter

≫   ≫   ≫   ≫   ≫   ≫   ≫   ≫   ≫

Radio and television broadcaster Art Linkletter has had a long and distinguished career celebrating the strength, humor, and beauty of the human spirit. In his early career he focused his energies on children, producing the television program "Art Linkletter's House Party" and such books as Kids Say the Darndest Things. *More recently he has turned his talents to inspirational speaking on the joys and pains of late life. His most recent book,* Old Age Is Not for Sissies, *has become a best-seller in the literature on aging. He is seventy-nine years old.*

W hen I think about growing older, I think there are many pluses. To begin with, you level out the violent swings of emotion that seem to pervade youth. Young people are either desperately miserable or gloriously happy. And, let's be frank about it, one of the things that levels out as you grow older is the sex drive, which, when you're young, obscures the rest of the horizon a good part of the time. As you get older it retreats to a more manageable level. That alone keeps you from liaisons and dangerous and risky things that can change your whole life when you're young; it can change your marriage, your career, your future. So as you age you begin to get some control of the libido.

Then, of course, there's the business of your ambition. Some people have a fierce and burning ambition, while others want job security and comfort. I was one of those who had a fierce ambition. I was never satisfied with what I had. I didn't have any goal to be the richest or the most powerful person; I just wanted to be better and better and better, and I moved often. I changed my mode of living drastically as I went on up the scale. And now, as I get older, I'm calming down a bit. Now that I've won the things I wanted I'm more patient, less of a workaholic, and not so much the constant, restless striver.

I do agree with the statement that growing old is one of the most surprising things that happens. I didn't give it any thought—as most people don't—because I was healthy, I was happy, and things were going along swimmingly. I was occupied with a career and a family—and all of a sudden I discovered one day that I had gotten old. In a family, you begin to realize you're old when your children become grandparents; that is a real reminder. I still thought of my son Jack as a little boy, but when he became a grandfather all of a sudden I realized that, yes, time has passed. Another reminder of my age was that I was on several boards of directors that had a mandatory retirement at seventy. When you are asked to leave a place on account of age, it's a very definite signal to you. Perhaps the most unpleasant part of it is that your circle of friends and close acquaintances and old-time buddies begins to thin out, because almost every month somebody you've known all your life dies. I have it happen every week almost. I just went to Danny Thomas's funeral; he was a friend of mine for forty years. Other friends of mine are deathly ill at this moment. All these things are unmistakable reminders that you are mortal and time is passing.

But I don't think much about death because I'm so busy and happy and excited. In fact, I've never had an age that has brought me up short, although I must say that approaching eighty gives me a little concern. Eighty seems to be, for me, not a big wall, but a strong reminder that most of my life has been lived. But I don't—I can't—worry about dying; I just am more concerned about seeing that my affairs are all in order, which is a good thing for the family. I would just hope that when my time comes it happens in a hurry.

One of the great rewards of growing older is that a person who grows old has experience. I think everybody over seventy-five should have an honorary doctorate degree in life, because you have lived it. Everyone over seventy-five has had triumphs, disasters, tragedies, stress, and all the other things that life brings. By the age of seventy, you learn to handle tough situations and to evaluate them properly. We older people just have a wealth of experience that you can get only by living. It's a big plus. We know a lot more about change than young people do, and this means that we know a lot more about life—because change, after all, is what life is all about.

The greatest changes that have occurred in my life happened when I was thrust into positions where I had to come up with solutions, or be an arbitrator in conditions where I found myself having to be the one who stopped the violence. I've become a kind of a pourer of oil on troubled waters. This occurred most dramatically when we were confronted with the death of my daughter, which was a watershed in my life. My beautiful nineteen-year-old-girl took her own life. This is the saddest and the most dramatic and the most unacceptable thing that can happen to a human being, to have your own child take her life or his life. At that point the family rallied around me, and I had to be strong and I had to find reasons that would be acceptable to the family as to why such a thing could happen. A few years later my thirty-two-year-old second son, Robert, was killed in a tragic automobile accident. Once again, the family rallied around me, and I had to be the one who tried to make sense out of this terrible loss. In struggling to do this, my life changed. I began, as a matter of fact, a new career as a lecturer, but I also began a new career as an adviser and a counselor to many, many people who were undergoing unbearable tragedies. From that moment on, I found that my mail, my personal contacts, have been filled with people who are losing something in life. They come to me as someone they know who has been through it. In tragedy you look for people who've had a similar tragedy because the truth of the matter is, no one else knows. There is no way for anyone to possibly understand what goes on in the mind and heart of someone who has an inconsolable loss, except someone who has had a similar one.

Out of those deaths and other tragedies that I've had in my life I've come to see that two things can happen to those who experience loss: You're either going to be diminished or you're going to be enhanced by facing up to your tremendous problems. It's up to you as to which is going to happen. Too many people who lose others— mothers, fathers, children, friends—become people who use grief as a tent pole for their life. They cherish it almost, they clutch it to them, they never let it go, and that grief becomes the impelling force for a negative, bitter, unhappy, vengeful, unforgiving life. Other people, like myself, use it as a springboard for being a better person and for enjoying life more and for appreciating life and all the good things in it as a counter to the other things that are going to happen.

After seventy-eight years of living, I'm convinced that the most important single thing that affects people— whether they're young or old—is their attitude. I've been very fortunate in that I've always, from my earliest days, been a hopeful and curious person. I always thought good things were going to happen to me, even though I had no reason to be particularly positive. I was abandoned as an orphan with no parents and no name. I was adopted by older people who were really old enough to be my grandparents; they were in their middle fifties. And they were poor, crippled, and not very well educated. So I grew up poor. I was a hobo, and I worked in many strange places to get by. I never remember being given anything, and yet out of that I always had the feeling that good things were going to come.

I'm pretty well convinced that those who tend to be happy are people who do what they can with what is possible and who just leave the rest to the Lord. You can sit around and worry about earthquakes and atom bombs until it obscures your entire life, until the worry just consumes you with fear or anger or just plain sadness.

As we get older we hear all these things like "over the hill," "out to pasture," "Oh, I should have done that when I was younger." Things like that can filter in and affect your attitude for the worse in a hurry. It's a constant battle to avoid them and to stress the good things, which include your family and whatever accomplishments you've had, or your friends or whatever health you have. In other words, "Emphasize the positive and eliminate the negative." That's not easy to do because we're surrounded by negatives. But we can do the best we can, and an attitude is generally derived from self-esteem, and self-esteem comes from a recognition that you have done the best you can with what you have. Not that you're richer or more powerful or more famous than anybody, or even the people you know, but that you did the best with what God gave you and what life gave you.

In all of this, humor is the lubricant you need to get through life, and it is particularly important as you age. If you can't laugh at your wrinkles and aches, you've got to scream. And poking fun at problems is the basis of a great deal of humor. In fact, it is the reputed reason why so many Jewish people have turned into great comedians and great humorists, because they come from a persecuted group who had to laugh at life or they would just have died. I have observed that this is true of any group of people who struggle. They have to laugh.

I like to think that every day some experience or some new acquaintance or some new challenge is going to change my life. In fact, I have a little poem-type philosophy that I sometimes use to conclude my talks: "I never want to be what I want to be, because there's always something out there yet for me. I get a kick out of living in the here and now, but I never want to feel I know the best way how. There's always one hill higher with a better view, something waiting to be learned I never knew. So 'til my days are over my prayer is, 'Never fill my cup, let me go on growing up.' "

William Manchester

❯ ❯ ❯ ❯ ❯ ❯ ❯ ❯ ❯

William Manchester, one of our nation's most distinguished writers, is adjunct professor of history and writer-in-residence at Wesleyan University and Fellow of Pierson College at Yale. His eighteen books, which have been translated into eighteen languages and braille, include The Death of a President, The Arms of Krupp, The Glory and the Dream, *and* The Last Lion, *a biography of Winston Churchill.*

I never even thought about my age until a couple of years ago. It never crossed my mind, just as dying doesn't cross my mind. I know it's going to happen, and there's nothing I can do about it but accept it. There are certainly some deprivations to growing older; I wouldn't deny that. I'm deprived, for example, of the great energy that youth has. Yet I look at students and I see how they waste that energy; they don't really accomplish very much with it.

I do not have the joy of young romance, which is terribly exciting, but it doesn't last for anybody, and I think probably a lot of the divorces arise from that fact—people think they've been cheated, you know. But in looking back old people have got to remember that romance also leads to a lot of heartbreak, and ambition does too. The things that can break your heart at my age are extremely few; they exist, but compared to the number of things that can happen to you when you're twenty-five or thirty, they are very small.

I'm also very much aware that I'm in a society in which I am a member of a minority group; most of the people are younger. The average age is now something like thirty or thirty-two. The advertising people are not aiming at people like me, and so there's a sense of isolation. But then a writer—as I am—is always isolated.

Still, there are many things about being older that are good. I find my life has become not only narrower and narrower, but also deeper and deeper. For example, I see fewer people and I read fewer books, but the books

I do read are very challenging, and the work that I do has more dimensions, more depth. I think the perspective of age, particularly for one who writes about history, is important.

I've noticed that my wife and I don't have much of a social life any more. For a long time here at Wesleyan, every Friday, Saturday, and Sunday evenings would be spent at faculty parties. Well, we don't get invited anymore because we don't entertain anymore. So I don't see very many people. And I don't travel the way I used to. I spend my time concentrated on one topic—the work that is before me—and that, I might say, is all that counts.

People find this difficult to grasp, but I receive absolutely no comfort or assurance from looking over my shoulder at work that I've done. All that matters to me is the blank page in front of me and filling it up. People don't understand that. They say, "But you've done so much." It doesn't matter. My ambition now is to finish up the third volume of my Churchill series, to finish that before I die. There are at least three other books I would like to write for fun if I have time, but I don't know.

I do know that I have no fear of death. That wasn't true when I was young, when I was a marine in World War II. I was wounded twice—the second time critically, on June 5, 1945. That morning is probably the pivotal date in my life because I came so very close to death. I was flown from Saipan to Hawaii on a C-47. Of the twelve critical cases on board, seven died en route; we had seven corpses when we arrived in Hawaii. The flight took twenty-four and a half hours, and we crossed the international date line. Well, having survived that, every day since then has seemed to me to be a gift that must be earned. Before then I squandered my time, but I don't squander it anymore. People who know me say they admire my self-discipline. They never say, "I admire your talent"; they say, "My, you're self-disciplined." That's something that all writers can count on. People say to us, "If only I had the time that you have." We all have the same amount of time, you know. So I reply that if we have a bad habit, we call it a bad habit, but if we have a good habit, we call it self-discipline, and so you form certain patterns. But for me, the inspiration behind those patterns was the discovery of my mortality when I had just passed my twenty-third birthday.

When I was discharged in San Diego on October 24, 1945, I was judged 100 percent disabled by wounds. It took a long time to come back. What saved me was that personally and professionally I am possessed by curiosity: I wanted to know how the war turned out, I wanted to know who won. If I was killed, I wouldn't know. But now I'm not at all worried about dying. I have lived a long and productive life. When the time comes, I'm ready to go. I remember Churchill in his last years saying, "A man can grow too old, and I am too old." Of course, he was in his nineties then. So I've come to peace with death. If I were told that I have six months to live, it would, as Samuel Johnson said, "concentrate the mind wonderfully." But I don't think that it will happen soon, because I have a grandmother who lived to be ninety-nine. I don't smoke or drink. I don't even drink tea or coffee, and I exercise, so I don't know how long I'm going to live.

One of the great advantages of this age is that I have fewer anxieties. There are so many anxieties when you're young. Of course you have more energy to deal with them, but you wonder, Am I ever going to reach a large audience with my books? Curiously, for a Depression child, I never thought very much about money, though I had to scrape for it. One way my life was changed by my wound on June 5, 1945, is that forever after I had a pension. When we married I was making eighty dollars a week as a newspaper reporter, and when I became a foreign correspondent it only went up to a hundred and ten dollars. But we always saved money, always. When I began to make money we already had evolved a rather spartan lifestyle. It's not spartan now—we have a home in Connecticut and a home in Florida—but I'm not much for money. I have always saved and invested money, and as a result I have an independent income. I'm autonomous, and that gives me a feeling of freedom. I am not responsible to anybody. When I was I hated it.

One thing that has changed for me is that when I grew up I felt there was an inner wisdom in the people. Ninety percent of the newspapers, for example, had opposed Roosevelt, but still he'd been elected four times. A key event in my life that changed my attitude was the defeat of Adlai Stevenson in 1952. This is when I began to lose faith in the wisdom of the people. I don't have any faith in them now. This is where I think Mencken is right; he said most people are boobs.

Something about age which you may have discovered is that when you are in your early sixties you have peers in power. But when you are really old, you are out of power. We're powerless and I'm very much aware of it. I'm sixty-nine and more and more the people I know are retiring, and when they retire they lose power. Even if I came to know him as well as I knew John Kennedy, I would have no influence with General Schwarzkopf. And when you pass that point, then the feeling of isolation increases. It is not all bad. For an artist, isolation is sometimes absolutely essential. This passing of the torch, this giving up of power, is one of the rites of passage of growing older.

Perhaps the greatest contribution of a liberal education is that it encourages you to keep an open mind. And it is a sign—a bad sign—of growing old when someone has increased his prejudices, and has certain fixed ideas not subject to change, which are based not on reason but are, in fact, irrational. I can speak critically of the younger generation, but there's a vast difference between that and the attitude of men I've met who just hate young people. I spoke of narrowing and deepening. I think the narrowing is inevitable, but if it's compensated for by greater depth, then you're growing. But there are old people who have grown narrower and shallower than they were. A continuing interest in what is new and what is happening, even when you don't fully understand it, is critical to living a rich and stimulating life.

Mary Martin

≫　　≫　　≫　　≫　　≫　　≫　　≫　　≫　　≫

I've always been rather wild. I wanted to be a performer from the time I was five. Now I'm in the latter part of my life, but I'm still learning, still learning. I learn every single day. Maybe that's because I don't feel any older. I may be seventy-four, but I really don't think I am.

Mary Martin died in November 1990, but she will live forever in our hearts as Peter Pan, the role she played so well

179

for more than forty years. It all started in Weatherford, Texas, when, at the age of five, a not-so-shy Mary Martin stood on the stage at the Fireman's Ball and sang "When Apples Grow on the Lilac Tree." After that, there was no question: theater was to be Mary Martin's calling. During her long career she played a number of memorable roles on Broadway, including Nellie Forbush in South Pacific *and Maria Von Trapp in* The Sound of Music.

Mary Martin made a number of comebacks in her career, including her starring role alongside Carol Channing in the play Legends *in 1986. But surely her most valiant comeback was in 1982, after a serious automobile accident in San Francisco nearly left her crippled for life.*

The auto accident in San Francisco was tragic, truly tragic, because I lost two good friends, but it did help to shape and strengthen my philosophy of life and perhaps my approach to aging. My manager was killed instantly and my dearest friend, Janet Gaynor, suffered injuries that were eventually fatal. At the time, the doctors feared I would be crippled for life.

My back was just a mess, so I bought myself a huge inner tube—the size of a Ford truck—and floated in the pool to exercise my arms and legs. I worked very, very hard in the pool, doing a variety of leg exercises over a long period of time. I worked hard to learn to walk again.

I remember at the time that I had one more show to do for "Over Easy" (the seniors program I did for PBS), and they said, "Don't worry, we'll bring you on the set in a wheelchair before anybody comes in and you can be seated on the couch." I said no. My entire family was there, and they said, "No, Mary is going to walk in." Yes, I said, I'm going to walk in with a walker for support because of the age group that is here. It shows that if I can do it, they can do it. So I walked in, sat down, and it was one of the greatest experiences of my life because it proved that almost anything can be done if you just don't stop working at it. If you've given in, you've had it.

After I was well into recovery I did a benefit for San Francisco General Hospital, where Janet and I were taken after the accident. I decided, from the beginning, that I wanted to do my flying routine at that event. It never occurred to me that it might be a problem to my body. I wasn't completely recovered, but I was well on the way. I've flown so many times—knocked out conductors and everything else—but some people urged me not to try it. They figured I was too old, or that I hadn't recovered enough yet. But I felt it was important for people to see a seventy-year-old woman flying at them from out of the dark—zoom, without a rehearsal! And that's the way it happened. I was up there, and it was at the end of the show, and the people were all staring up at me with their mouths open—and of course I'm throwing fairy dust like mad and it's in their noses and their hair, their eyes and their mouths. But by the time they left, they knew that if they believed in something, it could be done. That was the reason I wanted to fly. I just thought, what more could you show?

One of my most treasured possessions is the book *Around the Year with Emmet Fox*, which was given to me by Janet. I especially like one passage in the book because it encapsulates my entire philosophy of life. It goes like this: "A centipede was quite happy until a frog in fun said, 'Pray, which leg comes after which?' This raised her mind to such a pitch, she laid distracted in the ditch, considering how to run." Isn't that wonderful! I love it. I love it. Every time I think of feeling sorry for myself, I think of that centipede. There are some people who would lay in the ditch and feel sorry for themselves, but not me. I say get up and do it. I think people often give in too quickly. It may take a doctor and a nurse to help you regain your health, but it takes yourself to say, "I'm going to do it."

Rollo May

❧   ❧   ❧   ❧   ❧   ❧   ❧   ❧   ❧

Rollo May, one of America's most distinguished therapists, is a humanist by temperament. He is committed to the basic principles that we are responsible for the lives we lead, and that we make choices in all things and must accept the consequences. The more we know about ourselves, the more fulfilling these choices can be. His many influential books include The Courage to Create, Love and Will, Man's Search for Himself, The Meaning of Anxiety, *and* Freedom and Destiny. *Writing, thinking, and theorizing*

184 · Rollo May

continue to dominate Rollo May's later years. He is eighty-two.

I n *The Courage to Create*, I tried to make the point that
all of us have the potential to be creative. I think the
later years ought to be the time when we enjoy the
creativity that we have. I've always felt that asking people if they are creative or not is a foolish question. The
question really ought to be put this way: What is it that
you make? What is it that you do? When we think in
those terms, then all of us are creative—we all do
things, make things.

The problem isn't that all of us aren't creative, but
that some of us are using our creativity more than
others. Some of us have developed the courage to use
what we have, while others have not. And the stumbling
block is fear, simply fear. Let's face it, creative tasks are
scary. It takes a throwing of one's self into it. When you
throw yourself into something completely, you run the
risk of failure. You are alone in the process, and this
requires solitude and courage.

One of the problems of living creatively in late life is
that it gets harder as you grow old. Thomas Mann once
said that writing is something that becomes more difficult the more you do it. This is because one's idea of
what's acceptable and what's not becomes more rarefied
when one gets older. You have higher standards, you
might say. So you have to work harder and harder the
older you get, which is the exact opposite of what we've
planned for.

But I feel very strongly that creativity keeps us fresh, even though it requires great discipline and struggle. Fresh is the word I use, not young. I don't see becoming young as desirable at all, because young people often don't have the creativity that we have as we grow older. Creativity keeps us fresh; it keeps us alive, keeps us moving forward. You are never fully satisfied; you are always working and reworking your art, your book, your garden, whatever. I don't buy this stuff at all about youth being the happy time. My youth was not, and I don't think other people's youths were so great either. I think the older we get, the fresher we ought to get. We face our fears. We tackle them head on. We have the courage to create.

People in their eighties I've talked with, like B. F. Skinner or Hannah Tillich, have told me that they have only two hours a day in which they can work creatively. The rest of the day they devote to busy work. So you have to plan your days properly and guard your working time—your prime time—very carefully. I stay in my studio each day for four hours, but the last hour and a half isn't worth very much. It was hard for me to accept, but what can I do? All I can do is make the most of the creative time I've got. So for two and a half hours I'm moving marvelously; the rest of the time I'm simply fiddling around. But I find joy in fiddling too. I have to accept the fact that I'm not a god. I have to accept my destiny. I have to accept the fact that I can only do creative work for a few hours a day, but that doesn't diminish one iota the joy I get from those two hours.

I don't believe in happiness, but I do believe in joy.

I don't seek happiness particularly, but I do seek joy. Joy is the feeling of exhilaration, the buoyancy that comes from creating something you are pleased with. When you are in a state of joy, you don't feel like eating and you don't feel like sex—all of these are put aside and you are in a state of complete excitement. Joy is not limited to the young; it is there for all of us.

As I have said many times over the years, all of us have to take responsibility for our lives. If we want to live joyful lives, we've got to work at it. When I contracted tuberculosis as a young man, I gave myself over to the physicians, did everything they told me to, but I wasn't getting any better. The X rays each month looked worse and worse. Then I realized that I've got to take responsibility for my recovery, that I'm the one who can tell whether I'm getting better or not, whether I'm energetic or whether I need to rest. I began to listen to my body and slowly I got better. I was very poor then; we had three children, and my wife and I had no money. I borrowed whatever I could from my friends, and it was such that I never got out of debt until I was fifty years old. But I still think that period of tuberculosis was the single most important experience in my life. I learned then that not only was I responsible for the disease, but I could stand up, I could fight back, I could creatively tackle my problem.

To this day I believe strongly that overcoming disease is a creative process. One of my lungs from the tuberculosis never came back fully, but I now ride my bike twenty-four miles a week, I swim, and I climb trees. I had to learn that health is not something that is given to you; it is something you have to achieve, which is why I see it as a creative process. You must learn to be sensitive to your strength, about when you need rest, what you can do, what you can't do, how you must exercise. All of these things are creative processes. Now I watch my health very closely. For one thing, I meditate. I eat with care. I watch my cholesterol. I make sure that I sleep at least seven and half hours a night, and I always take a half hour nap after every lunch. If I stopped these things I would, in two or three months, be a wreck. Those things are necessary for the life I love.

I believe that one lives as long as one has something to contribute. All the creative people that I've known have died once they stopped being creative. Now, I may have the cart before the horse there—they may have stopped their creativity because they sensed that something was being blocked—but I have this prejudice that we live so long as we have something important to say. Once we've said it, we die. Kierkegaard died in his middle forties, but he said what he needed to say. Pascal died in his late fifties, but he said what he needed to say. So I don't know that time is so crucial in this matter of death. Does it make a difference whether you die in your thirties or in your eighties? It seems to me there is an element of eternity and you ought to judge these things not by the number of years somebody lived, but by the concept of eternity. One can live an eternal life at thirty, or one can live such a life and die at ninety. I hope, incidentally, that I don't get too old. I hope I will die with a heart attack, say, in my late eighties. I'd like to just faint and go out. I don't dread it at all. What there is, if anything, after death I don't know.

One of the saddest things about growing old in America is that we don't honor the old at all. We don't revere older people nearly as much in this society as Indians, Native Americans, other societies have done. Greek society, for example, revered the old. Now, I think this is a sign of the decadence of our age, that we no longer value, no longer see the contribution of, older people. We worship youth, and I think that is the craziest thing I ever heard of. I never want to live my youth over again, and I never met anyone who really did. It's just a figment of one's imagination. But I think that our civilization is now going through a radical decadence and the real question will be, will there be a renaissance or will we blow ourselves up?

I really think creativity is the answer to aging, and by creativity I mean listening to one's own inner voice, to one's own ideas, to one's own aspirations. It may be social work. It may be gardening. It may be building. But it must be something fresh, something new, some idea that takes fire—this is what I'd like to see among older people. When Matisse was in bed and couldn't get up the last year of his life, he found something creative to do. He got himself a pair of scissors and made all these cutouts in paper, and they are fantastically beautiful. I love them very much. I have a reproduction of one in my office, leaning up against one of the walls to remind me of what old people can do in their last years.

When I die, I will surely be unhappy that I haven't done as much reading of Greek mythology as I would have liked. I get so involved when I'm reading Greek myths that I move very, very slowly. I don't turn many pages, but it's a wonderful joy to me. Now, that is what age ought to do for us. Sure, you don't remember names so well, you can't run this or that marathon, your joints are stiffer . . . all this is certainly true. But at the same time, you have a lot of experience you can call upon, you have a kind of wisdom that leaves out the details and simply goes straight for the important things. This is the meaning of the wisdom of the ages.

Donald Ross

Rosario Mazzeo

⋙ ⋙ ⋙ ⋙ ⋙ ⋙ ⋙ ⋙ ⋙

Rosario Mazzeo speaks lovingly of his lifetime careers of sight and sound—photography and music. His professional life was as a bass clarinetist and Personnel Manager of the Boston Symphony Orchestra. Yet his reputation wasn't limited to the world of music. Many exhibits of his powerful photographs of nature and foreign landscapes reflect both his passion and reverence for life. Now in his eightieth year, Rosario Mazzeo's "Santa Claus-like beard," sparkling eyes and friendly smile match his warm and animated conversation.

I don't play the clarinet any more. I stopped playing about fifteen years ago. I've played 6,000 concerts with the symphony and another 1,000 or so solo performances and chamber music concerts, so I've had my fill. You see, I have always despaired of hearing players taper off. I can't tell you how many times I've heard players perform who shouldn't. They were past their time and I vowed that when my time came I would stop. So I stopped when I reached that point, when it was no longer possible for me to practice every day. You just can't play the clarinet well unless you play every day and keep your arms and hands in condition.

But there's no sadness, none at all. I had a wonderful time. I loved it. I look back on it with great joy, and I still enjoy listening to recordings of myself. But I don't find myself thinking that I'd like to do it again. I wouldn't. It was done, it was right for then, I'm happy that I did it well, and that is enough. If I sat back looking regretfully at my past, then my future would look a little pale. And the future is what I'm living for, not the past. The moment you start looking back, trying to remake the past, you're taking away from the energy you need to live the future.

I love to walk. I try to walk at least three to ten miles every day. Walking certainly has been one of my lifelong passions. I don't think there's a day that I don't walk some miles. I've had fairly extensive times of walking, too. Once I walked from Massachusetts to Canada over the Green Mountain Ridge, carrying a clarinet on my back the whole way. That's probably a world record for carrying a clarinet on your back! That took me a month. I've also made long walks in Iceland, California, New England, Maine—all sorts of places.

Walking is superb! You have a different equilibrium when you're walking. You're aware of everything that's around you, but you aren't just staring all the time. You're going along thinking and then you just look and see this and that around you, and then your mind turns towards other things. You can do long-range thinking when you walk. An idea can sort of spin around in your head as you walk along.

You see, I'm not a religious person. I think if I were asked to state my religious belief I would say it was just nature. My outdoor life has been such a part of me because I love to be there and the world is very clear when I'm there. It's not for me to try to understand such things as how we came into being. I'm here, the natural world is around me, and I think the more we partake of each other, the better off we are.

In Maine once I was walking part of the Appalachian Trail in the early summer. I was way off in nowhere, deep in the woods, and I came to an opening and there was a fellow sitting there, an older woodsman. I stopped to chat with him. He was sitting on a log with his rucksack and a couple of other possessions around him. We talked about this and that and then I asked him, "Where are you bound?" "Well," he said, "I'm not going anywhere. I'm right here now. I'm actually going up to the other end of the lake; we're going to lumber up there this winter. I'm a log cutter and I go up there and lumber. George is going to pick me up sometime soon." I said, "Who is George, and what time is he supposed to be here?" "Well," he said, "he's my foreman and he's going to be along some time this fall." And I said, "This fall! Why, that's months away. How long have you been waiting here?" "I've been here only a week so far," he told me.

My encounter with this woodsman reminded me of the fact that we measure time differently at different spaces in our lives. When I was a youngster my mother said, "We'll do this or that next week on Tuesday," and it seemed that next week never came. A week at that age was something unbelievable. Now, at the age of eighty, time has a different pace and meaning and importance.

Today I am essentially free of any kind of formal schedule, so I spend my time taking photographs, walking, or being with friends and family. I've cut my music teaching back to two days a week. But I'm not finished with life so I have great aspirations for the future, however long it may be. I hope I can go full strength right to the end. Of course, we don't always have a choice. My end might come lingeringly or rather abruptly, but if I keep my mind on it, then I can't enjoy today. So I put my mind on today and let tomorrow happen. Our whole thinking should be in terms of forward. We all want to have nostalgic looks into the past, but in a way that's only firing us up more for the future, because the more you look back and see all that was happy in the past, you say, "I'd like to have more of that—how do I get it?" Well, you get it by living. Enjoy today, do all the things that you're capable of doing with fervor and everything else will take care of itself.

Eve Merriam

᚛   ᚛   ᚛   ᚛   ᚛   ᚛   ᚛   ᚛   ᚛

I 'm seventy-four, and people are always amazed when they hear that. They say, "Oh, you look so young." But that is one of those jokes. You could be in your coffin and they'd say you don't look it. But the fact is, one does take it as a compliment. My hair, for example, is not entirely gray yet, and I like it when people say, "What lovely hair. You're so vigorous and your body is just in great shape." It pleases me, yes it does.

Eve Merriam was born and raised in Philadelphia, the youngest child of Russian-born parents who owned a chain of women's dress shops. Books and reading were an important part of her youth, and the written word has captivated her ever since. Over the years, she has found several avenues of expression as a writer, most notably as a poet and playwright. She has written over fifty books of prose and poetry for both adults and children, including Fresh Paint, Mommies at Work, *and* The Inner City Mother Goose.

I can't really praise age. That would be unfair, because all of us would like to be immortal and live forever. We always think that aging, as well as death, is what happens to other people. I think what has come upon me is a very slight degree of tranquility toward the future, a sort of "*Que sera, sera,*" what will happen in the future will happen. I no longer feel I can control all the destiny that there is. So age tends to make me a little more humble toward the universe. Remember the great story about Margaret Fuller when she exclaimed, "I accept the universe!" and Ralph Waldo Emerson responded, "Madam, you damn well better."

So I think one comes to accept aging. Yet there's a shyness that I find that I never had before in life. A certain shyness about, "Oh, dear, I'm an old lady now, my hair has turned gray, will young people want to be with me?" Even though I've spent all my life with younger people because the bulk of my work is in the theater and poetry. There is that certain shyness that I find. I don't know whether this pertains to other older people too. I don't know whether I still belong in the magic circle of immortality or not. And I want to be part of the dance.

I think I'm sort of inclined to agree with Lillian Hellman that one gets older but not necessarily wiser. Perhaps one of the few good things about getting older is that life becomes so precious on a day-to-day basis. I think I've always had a certain amount of daily joy, but now I find it even more so—the sight of a clear sky in New York, which doesn't come all that often, or being out in the country, or right now in the spring, in April, where the trees are just the greenest they've ever been, and even the colors that people wear. I feel the senses become heightened. I know that some scientists think that our senses become dimmed with age, but I think it's just the reverse.

I think that a love for the ordinary is what is most important as one ages, not for the extraordinary. There are always trips to Bali or Yokohama or Paris, but to get the joy out of the daily-ness, that's what struck me when I hit my sixties. I thought, Good heavens, I'm getting so much pleasure out of my breakfast. I didn't know grape-fruit juice could taste so good. This is really amazing. It's as though some kind of slight film over the world has been stripped away and there is now a clarity that one didn't have before. I'm a big walker—I love to walk—and the rhythm of my body walking just seems to give me more pleasure now. And I feel that the visual sense is heightened, despite using glasses for reading. I think the sense of smell, even though I've heard that it dims, is for me sharper and clearer. Smell is the most evocative of memories, and we have more memories as we age, naturally. The sense of touch becomes very, very significant. I've always had a lot of plants in my apartment, but I think the pleasure that I get now out of pruning them and trimming them is even more. So I'm deliberately talking about ordinary things, and that is something that I want very much to pass on to younger people and to children. In fact, I did a book for children called *Unhurry Harry*, in which the main character is very slow because he's always savoring all of his five senses.

I have finally learned to pare away things that don't interest me that much. There's no question that time is more precious now and I really hate to waste it. I used to be the kid who would go to three parties every night—heaven forbid that I would miss something. Now I don't do that. I pick and choose very carefully. And I feel the same way with seeing people. I really only want to see people I can get something out of. I'm looking for a meeting of minds, not that we necessarily have to feel the same way about politics or the social order, but so that I can get something out of the experience.

I suppose you'd say it's a cleaning out time for me. I'm even cleaning out the clothes closets. I used to be a fashion editor, so I know pretty much the sort of things that are becoming to me, and now I'm clearing out clothes and trying to clear out clutter from my desk— papers that I don't really need. There is a very good feeling about cleaning up debris.

But, you know, there's a lot of debris you can never fully get rid of. I never quite believe those people who say, "I regret nothing." I can't imagine that there wouldn't be regrets unless one is the sort of person who's never done anything. And all my life I've been very impulsive. I once got married after I knew somebody for three weeks; it was not a marriage that lasted forever. I will give things away on impulse. I will write on impulse. I've always done that, so I've made many errors of judgment in the course of my life. When I look back there are many things that I would have done differently. I wish that I had my children earlier and wish that I had more of them. I was thirty-five when my first son was born, and then I wanted to have children quick, so the second was born just ten and a half months later. I wish that my last marriage, which was the happiest marriage of my life, had come earlier. I wish a lot of things, I regret a lot of things. But on the other hand, there are so many highs that I've had.

I had my most passionate marriage when I turned sixty, so I think that older women have the ability to be passionate forever and ever. It's easier for women than for men, because I think we find sensuality, as well as sexuality, in different areas. I think that the fact that we deal with children, that we deal with the domestic as well, lends an extra edge to the sexual and the sensual. But our society really doesn't like to think of older ladies as sexy. Nobody wants to think that there are women out there howling like banshees and having relationships with younger men, which is always threatening. We're a very conservative society, and always have been, so we put things in slots. You know, there's young love, there's adolescence, then you get married, then you raise your family, and then you sort of turn into a walking television box and just sit there like Darby and Joan. It's possible that Darby and Joan had a terrific sex life. I'm sure William Blake and his wife did. I knew Dr. W. E. B. Du Bois, the great African-American scholar, and when he was ninety-six he would kiss you and you knew you had been kissed. And certainly somebody like Louise Nevelson exuded sexuality until she was very, very far along in her life. Or what about Martha Graham? I loved her vanity of wearing little white gloves so that you wouldn't notice the veins on her hand. I think she was a very sexual person. I love feisty, sexy old ladies; they make me very happy.

Dick Munro

≫   ≫   ≫   ≫   ≫   ≫   ≫   ≫   ≫

July, 1990. Time Life Building, Rockefeller Center, New York City.

At sixty years of age, Dick Munro has just taken official retirement from his powerful position as chief executive officer of Time Warner Inc. Munro joined Time, Inc. in 1957 as part of Time *magazine's circulation department. His career has included a variety of management positions, eventually bringing him into the CEO leadership role. Concurrent with making the commitment to serve in that job, he also planned for his retirement ten years hence, claiming that a decade of such enormous responsibility would be an adequate and sufficient length to serve. "Then," he claimed, "it will be time for me to do some other things."*

You are interviewing me after having been retired since May; it's been only two months. And these past two months have been rather hectic, because a lot of stuff that I was committed to prior to my retirement I'm still committed to. My life has not changed a hell of a lot yet, but it will. I know it will. But this is an awkward time in my life where a lot of things are not yet sorted out.

I'm sort of semi-retired. I am no longer the chief executive of Time Warner, but I am still involved with the company from a distance. I remain on the board of directors and I chair the executive committee, but I am not involved in the day-to-day operations or in running this company any longer, so I am rid of a great deal of pressure. I don't have that kind of pit in the bottom of my stomach that I used to have.

My feeling is, having been a chief executive for ten years, that's every bit as long as anybody should try and do that job. I think the younger people coming up have more energy. They're very, very bright, they're aggressive, and I know I'm not nearly as quick at sixty as I was at fifty. So I think part of the wisdom of getting older is to recognize you're getting older, that you weren't the same person you were ten or fifteen or twenty years ago.

I said ten years ago when I was fifty that I was going to retire when I was sixty. I had ten years to prepare for it, but I don't think you can ever really prepare. You try to, and you talk to people who have been through it, but until you actually do it, until that day when you don't have to wake up to catch the 6:02 train, it isn't a reality you're ever fully prepared for. That's particularly the case when you've worked for the same company for thirty-five years, in the same building, and caught the same train for all those years. It's something I approached with caution and, honestly, some trepidation. It's not traumatic, but it *is* a jolt.

I haven't yet experienced the full impact because I'm involved in so many things with other corporations. I still have a fairly full schedule, although it's more relaxed. The pressure of being a chief executive has been removed. I didn't lay awake nights and all that business, but when you are the boss there is a constant concern about what's going on in your corporation's life. It's not that I'm not concerned any longer, but it's no longer my responsibility. When that is removed from your shoulders, it makes a dramatic change in your life. For example, I've been home a couple days a week and my wife, Carol, gets a kick out of this. She says—jokingly I hope!—"You're not hanging around here!"

I certainly am not of the disposition to sit in a rocking chair now; I'm only sixty. I'm still relatively young and quite healthy at the moment, and I've got lots of energy. I'm an active kind of person. I hope there comes a time later this year where I get into a pattern that lets me play a little bit more tennis than I've played in the last number of years and perhaps do some reading that I haven't done.

One thing I am aware of is that once you step back from being the chief executive, you're out of the game. I mean the baton has been passed, there's a new management. And though as a director I will observe this new management and hope to be asked my counsel occasionally, I'm not waiting for the phone to ring. Those of us who have had these kinds of jobs realize that once you give up that job, you give it up. American business is on such a fast track that my successors really don't have time to call up Dick Munro anymore. Those days are gone, and that's how it should be. But at the same time I would hope that occasionally my colleagues would call on me if they think I can be of help. And I would hope that within the boardroom occasionally I can ask a good question and hopefully, if asked, can supply a good answer. But again, in a corporation, either you're in it up to your neck or you're not in it, and from now on I'm not in it.

The people I worry about more than myself are the ones who built their entire life around being the chief executive officer; you know the power of that office— the limousines, the planes, the people waiting on you and all that. A certain percentage of us did have all those perks and took it all rather seriously, and once that's gone and the phone doesn't ring, you're kind of on your own out there. That can be horrendously traumatic for people. But those CEOs are in the minority. I think most of us have other lives and are not completely dependent upon the executive suite. Those who are, God, I feel sorry for them, because it's going to be a very tough life. If they took all this stuff that surrounds us seriously, they're in trouble, because when it's gone, it's gone. I've heard stories about wives of CEOs who go berserk when they suddenly realize the airplane's not there to take them where they want to go. I never used those kinds of perks, but for people who have, it can be very difficult.

I see nothing all that traumatic ahead for me. In fact, I'm looking forward to the slower pace. My wife and I have not traveled as much as we would like to, what with raising our children and all, but now all our children are either out of college or in college. So I see my retirement as an opportunity for us to do a little traveling. I know we'll spend more time at our summer place, which means we'll be up there in the spring and the fall. It'll be a much more relaxed life, and we'll have a chance to see more of each other—I hope that's good. I hope Carol thinks it's good. [Laughs.]

I'm not really worried that I will be bored in my retirement. I doubt that I'll look around and say, "Gee, what am I going to do now," because if I listed off the organizations that I'm a part of, you wouldn't believe it. I've still got plenty to do. But it would be premature to tell you how I'm going to get through this retirement business because I'm new to it. Retirement, like most subjects, is a tough one to generalize upon. I've approached it with my eyes open, aware that there could be some pitfalls, knowing that the

Munro family life will change now and I think we're
ready for that. As a matter of fact, we're not only
ready, we're looking forward to it.

*Note: On September 26, 1991, we met up with Dick Munro
in New York City to see how he was handling his first year
of retirement.*

As someone said to me the other day, I'm flunking
retirement! It's as big an adjustment as I anticipated it
to be. It's difficult to retire. I don't miss being a CEO
one iota, but I had really anticipated that I would have
more time for myself. As you know, I am involved in an
enormous number of things—far too many. I've been
unable to sever some of those ties, and people keep
coming after me to do other things. I have a difficult
time saying no, so I find myself running around at
perhaps even a more hectic pace—even though it is far
less structured—than before. But no one is making me
do this; it's no one's fault but Dick Munro's.

Subconsciously, I think I'm afraid of not having anything to do. I'm overcompensating for that by answering
the phone and saying yes to a number of things I just
shouldn't do. There will come a time when the phone
will ring and I'll say, "No, I can't do that."

Don't get me wrong, I love my life. I love what I'm
doing. I love not doing what I used to do. My only
problem is that I'm overdoing it. I'm just doing too
damn many things and I should fix that!

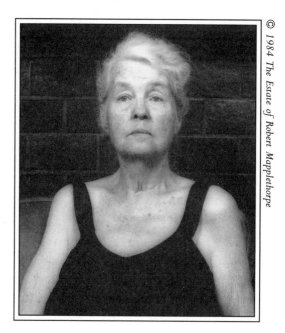

Alice Neel

≫   ≫   ≫   ≫   ≫   ≫   ≫   ≫   ≫

D o you know what happens to a lot of artists? They get to be forty or fifty and they're set and that's it. They just keep repeating the same thing. That's what most people do when they get old. I'm not like that, no. In fact, if I deserve credit for anything, I deserve credit for being able to paint an original interpretation of something at the age of eighty-four.

A sketchy overview of Alice Neel's life includes a suicide attempt, confinement in a mental hospital, desertion by her husband, and an effort to raise two sons by herself. Once a drug-crazed sailor destroyed all of her paintings, yet she never stopped making her art. In her art as in her life, Alice Neel has been fiercely independent. During the many years when abstract expressionism, pop art, and minimalism attracted the art world's attention, her portraits, which now number over 500, were largely ignored. Only the past twenty-five years have brought her recognition.

Alice Neel was feisty, outspoken, and determined to do her work. Cataracts, diminished hearing, diabetes, and a pacemaker didn't seem to get in her way. She just wouldn't allow it. She died in October 1984.

I have a susceptibility to nervous breakdowns and nervous disorders. I was dying of that. It used to be that about every three months I would faint. But then it got to the point in 1980 when I fainted three times in a month. So my son, who is a doctor in Vermont, came down to see what was what and he realized that I was dying. He took me up to Mass General and right in front of all the doctors I had one of my fainting attacks and my heart went down to forty beats a minute. I could have died right there. But they wheeled me in and gave me a pacemaker and I am much better now. I never faint anymore, but the doctors asked me to work less each day.

I actually work very fast and with such intensity that in two hours I have said about everything that I have to say for that day. So I'm really not cutting back at all. I never saw myself as a workaholic. I never was one of those idiots, although I hesitate to say that because one of my favorite writers, Thomas Mann, went to his studio just like one went to the office. And I must admit that if you work every day, if you shut yourself up, if you don't have an idea you'll eventually get one. All you can do if you think you are an artist and you have conviction is to work. If you work, you keep on developing. If you don't, that's it. Many artists are finished at fifty. Of course, when Titian was in his nineties he was still painting great pictures. And Cézanne, of course, painted great works until his death at the age of sixty-eight.

I painted a nude of myself at eighty. I didn't paint it to shock; I did it because my own face bores me. I can't bear my little Anglo-Saxon face. But with my whole body, there are lots of strange things going on. My flesh is falling off the bones, I have bad feet and a prehensile big toe, and there's a leg there somewhere. It's frightful, but as a work of art it's gorgeous. So I made myself as is, just like I do other people. I'd rather be called insane at eighty than be called vain making myself beautiful, you know.

I'd rather be called an insane old woman than a normal one. That right there is the secret of my success.

Dr. Norman Vincent Peale and Ruth Peale

⟫   ⟫   ⟫   ⟫   ⟫   ⟫   ⟫   ⟫   ⟫

Norman Vincent Peale is the author of the best-seller The Power of Positive Thinking *and is one of the most influential religious leaders in the world. At ninety-three, he is also one of America's most sought after speakers. Ruth, his wife of sixty-one years, is eighty-five years old.*

NORMAN VINCENT PEALE: Ruth and I walk a mile, two miles—even three miles—a day when the weather is good. We'll walk a long time saying nothing to each other but communing just the same. I tell you, when I was single and pastor of a church in Syracuse, there were many student activities that I was involved in. One Sunday after church I was holding a committee meeting of students in the front part of the sanctuary. It was a beautiful day in October—golden light, changing leaves, and all that. Suddenly the door opened with a bang, and a girl stood framed in the doorway. She was impatient that the meeting had gone on so long because she was waiting for a girlfriend who was in the meeting. I didn't know this girl framed in the doorway—I'd never seen her before, knew nothing about her—but I knew in that instant that she was the girl for me. It took me about two years to persuade her of that fact. We've been married now for sixty-one years. We can go long periods of time in a car, driving without saying anything, but we're communicating. If you have a love between people and perfect harmony, you don't need words to say something.

RUTH PEALE: When Norman and I aren't sitting together quietly in perfect harmony [laughs], we're either writing or talking our way through life. We publish books, and Norman spends two to three days a week speaking to national or regional business conventions. We have a message that we believe in, and we write it and we speak it.

NORMAN: I'm ninety-three-years-old now, and I'd say that for the past fifty years or more I've been saying much the same thing: Don't be defeated by your troubles. You have power over them if you only realize it, because you have a brain and you can think. The brain can think its way through any problem or any difficulty. So believe in yourself and your sovereign worth.

Someone who taught me a great deal about positive thinking and aging was an old friend of mine, the late Frank Bering. Frank was the general manager of the old Sherman House at Clark and Randolph streets in Chicago. I speak at many business conventions and Chicago is a convention city, so I was in and out of there often. Frank came from a little town down near Cincinnati where my family originated, and he had a sentiment for hometown boys, so he never charged me for a room in the Sherman House, nor for a meal. Naturally, I always stopped there when we were in Chicago. Well, one day I was speaking to a convention at lunch and they had about 1,200 people there, and Frank, at that time, was eighty-seven years of age—much older than I. I was about sixty at the time. He was supervising this meal, and I said to him, "Frank, how old are you, anyway?" He said, "What's the matter? Don't you like your room and isn't the service good in this hotel?" I said, "It's fine." "Well," he said, "why do you ask my age?" I said, "I know it anyway because you went to high school with my mother." "If you knew it," he said, "why do you bring it up?" And then he came over and punched me in the chest. (That was his sign, his way of showing affection, a resounding punch in the chest.) He said, "Young fella" (and that went over big with me), "I'll give you a word of advice. Live your life and forget your age." Now, I took that to heart. So I stopped thinking in terms of aging, and I don't think of myself in those terms today. I've always done what I'm doing now, and I intend to keep on doing it until the Great Referee says, "You're out."

RUTH: That settles with me perfectly, although I would add that to age well you need one other thing: creative innovation. It isn't enough just to work until you die. You have to work at getting better too. That is why I like to arrange think sessions, to get a group of people together to figure out a better way of doing something. There's always a new idea. Creative innovation keeps you young.

NORMAN: I've always said that there are only two ways you can think, either negatively or positively. The person who thinks negatively is doing a very dangerous thing, because he or she is sending out negative thoughts into the world and conditioning that world negatively. There is a law called the law of attraction, in which like attracts like. If you constantly send out negative thoughts, you're going to draw back to yourself negative results. Thoughts reproduce themselves in kind, so if you deal in negative thoughts, you attract negative results. However, if you think positively, you tend to attract positive results. So if you want to be a negative old person, negative people will find their way to you; if you want to be a positive old person, positive people will come to you. The secret to overcoming loneliness is to learn how to be a positive and entertaining person.

I like to feel that positive thinking helps to create an attitude in your mind that is very different from a negative attitude. You view things very differently if you have a positive reaction. It can be just as simple as getting up on a rainy day and being thankful that it's raining because you needed some rain. If you continue to think positively, you can accomplish a great deal more.

To every disadvantage, there is a corresponding advantage. If you think that's true, then when the disadvantage comes, you should say to yourself, Now, what is the corresponding advantage in this disadvantage? You'll always find one. If you hurt your knee and find that you can't play tennis, realize that now you have an opportunity to learn golf!

I'm a great believer in the fact that you can think your way into health and well-being. I have to admit that I was given a healthy body, but I was consulting with a doctor the other day and he wanted to know whether I wished to have him prescribe some pills for me. I said, "Oh, no, I don't intend to put any chemicals in my body. If I have a little pain here or a little pain there, I will endure the pain rather than having you prescribe for me a chemical that might change the balance in my bloodstream." Well, he looked at me with astonishment. He said, "Boy, you're all right, and you're going to live to a ripe, old age."

I think if you continue to work your mind, your mind will work as long as you work it. If you come to age sixty-five and you say, "Now I'm retired and I'm an old man," or "I'm an old woman," and sit down, your mind will accept your evaluation of yourself and act accordingly. It will get old and tired and sleepy. I still speak, and I speak without notes or without any assistance, and I find that on the platform before an audience, at ninety-three years of age, I can be just as alive as I was at forty. I still get the invitations to speak, so audiences and chairmen of committees must feel that I can deliver.

RUTH: There is a phenomenon in our country about retirement: certain people are being forced into early retirement. I think it's essential that if anybody is forced into that kind of a situation that they immediately go and find some creative activity in which they can engage. Unless they get into an activity that demands of them a thought process which brings out new ideas, they will deteriorate; it's just that simple. I know of many organizations where they want that kind of volunteer help. We've gone into senior citizen communities where they have developed a wide range of activities. One community we visited realized that they needed to have a place in that city where they could rent out various health equipment. If somebody was ill, maybe they needed a hospital bed or a wheelchair for a while. Well, a very successful retired businessman heard about the need and organized things until he had a big warehouse full of equipment. In other words, he created a nonprofit business to serve his community, and he did a marvelous job. Now there is an example of positive thinking and creative innovation in action.

NORMAN: As I said earlier, there is an advantage to every disadvantage. And aging has a few advantages that I never quite expected. I was, for example, on a Madison Avenue bus one time and a teenage boy said to me, ''Sir,

I wish you would take my seat." I said, "Well, thank you very much, but I can stand and you've got the seat, so enjoy it." "No," he said. "Sir, you've got to sit down here. If I went home and told my mother that there was an elderly gentleman standing and I didn't give him a seat, she would criticize me and you don't want me to get on bad terms with my mother, do you?" And I said, "Well, since you put it that way, I'll cooperate." I sat down and I said to him, "This is one of the advantages of being old. I meet a nice teenager like you who is a perfect gentleman. And," I said, "always be that way." So he and I parted friends, and I never forgot him, never forgot him, nice boy.

The main thing in life is, I think, to be sensitive to other people. I was riding on a subway in New York one day and I saw an elderly couple sitting across from me. They were both staring ahead, not saying anything to each other. Then I saw the lady reach out and touch her husband's hand. It touched me so much that I began to cry. [Tears come to his eyes.] As you can see, it still affects me.

RUTH: It breaks you up when you talk about it. I remember the time we were driving down Fifth Avenue together and we stopped at a red light and I said, "Norman, look over here to the right. There is a couple having a terrible argument; you can tell from the expressions on their faces and their looks at each other. Let's start praying for them right away." Even after the red light changed and we moved on in the traffic, Norman and I, together, prayed for that couple in the street.

When I get into a Fifth Avenue bus, I find myself looking all over the bus at faces. So many faces these days are tense or worried. You don't find many that give a feeling of serenity, and so I always pray for people. My friend Frank Laubach, author of *Prayer: The Mightiest Force in the World*, talks about shooting prayers at people. I believe in that. And so, if I'm riding on a bus, I spend my time shooting prayers at people in the bus.

NORMAN: One of the dearest friends I ever had was a fellow in Bellefontaine, Ohio, where we lived for a short time. I worked for him after school and on Saturdays. His name was Emil Geiger, and he ran a clothing establishment for men. And he said, "Norman, I got a bunch of suits that are a little bit out of style, but they're good quality. I'd like to load them into a wagon and have you go around and peddle them to farmers in the neighborhood." (A horse-drawn wagon, it was.) So he put them in and he said, "Now, never lie to any customer. Tell him the truth about this merchandise, and you're going to meet fine people. There's nothing greater than the Ohio farmer. Just go and love them." Years later I was speaking in my church one day in New York, and I looked out and saw this old man down there and I thought, "I know him; who is he?" I got close to him afterwards, and it was Emil Geiger. He went into my office and he said, "Boy, you're handing out the right stuff, because the people that are listening to you have all kinds of troubles. Just love 'em." And he said to me, "I love you, son." And I said, "I love you, Emil." I never saw him again, but he taught me that something is lovable about every human being. Ruth and I have tried to predicate our lives on helping people to endure the pain of human existence.

RUTH: I asked Norman not too long ago, "Norman, are we going to work all our lives?" He said, "Yes." Just as simple as that. And we don't chafe under it. We enjoy it; we're happy. We don't do any partying anymore. Now, in our early life, down in New York City, I did a great deal of entertaining. But we now feel as though that's not the way to spend our energies, so we work all the time. Every once in a while I will say, "Norman, we haven't been to a movie or the theater in years." And he says, "That's right, I'll take you soon." But that "soon" hasn't happened yet!

Jason Robards

❧ ❧ ❧ ❧ ❧ ❧ ❧ ❧ ❧

Ever since his first stage appearance at the Delyork Theatre in Rehoboth Beach, Delaware, in July 1947, Jason Robards has been delighting audiences with his charming, attractive, and dignified style. He is the recipient of an Emmy, an Obie, a Tony, and two Oscars for best supporting actor. He is sixty-nine years old.

I 'll tell you something. I went on a train last year to New York, instead of driving down from Connecticut, and I really looked like a million bucks. I had to go in to the city to do something, so I had on a blue suit, vest, tie, and a snap brim hat; I really looked good. I got on the train and the conductor came down and he punched the thing and he said, "That will be three dollars." (Usually the fare's nine, ten dollars.) I said, "Oh, really?" He said, "Here." I said, "All right." I knew the guy was a fool; I looked on the ticket, and he had punched "senior citizen, disabled." Disabled? I've never looked so good in my life! So when I got to Grand Central, I said, "You know something? I'm going over and buying my ticket now so I won't have to buy it tonight when I go home." When I bought the ticket I said, "I want a senior citizen ticket." I didn't say "disabled" because I was walking. [Laughs.] And the guy says, "Let me see your driver's license." He didn't believe me, so I had to pull out my driver's license and that card that they give you at sixty-five with the red, white, and blue on it. He begrudgingly gave me a three-dollar ticket. So you see, the conductor and the clerk at Grand Central had a completely different opinion of me. Actually, I was quite proud to have to bring out the license and the card for old age. I've really arrived, haven't I?

The way I see it, life is like a hotel. We've all got to check in and we've all got to check out. It's not a permanent place, this earth. So I've got to take each day and enjoy it as I can, as much as I can. And I do enjoy where I live and I enjoy my wife and I love my children. I go to Dartmouth—make a round trip, I don't care—just to go up and have dinner with my daughter if she wants me that weekend. We've been working on our house, which we love to do. Yesterday I was out doing a lot of pruning of roses and things that I'd never do ordinarily. I find that I have much more time to spend with my children and my home, and I like that part about getting older.

I find that I am acting kinder and more forgiving to people these days. I'm not condemning, not as judgmental as I was. I find that's a praiseful thing. Instead of passing judgment or passing anger, I work to turn my negative thoughts and experiences into something else. I find that I'm mellowing a bit. And I'm more trusting of myself, more confident in my abilities. I remember, for example, that on the opening day of *The Iceman Cometh* I was terrified. I had some strange feeling that this play signified a milestone. So I wrote myself a letter the day before we opened and mailed it to the theater. It said in it, "Dear Jason, Trust yourself." Then I signed it, "Love, Jason." That's all I had in it. It was sitting on my dressing room table when I came to open the play; it got me through that performance. But now I don't have to write that letter anymore, and that's a great relief. I've got trust in myself, both personally and professionally. Now I find that if I do certain steps in my work, I don't have to do anywhere near the research that a lot of younger people do. I count on my experience and my imagination. That there is a big plus to maturity.

Humor is very important in my life, and I know that came from my dad. I'll never forget this: I was picking my nose as a little kid and I was rolling it between my thumb and my forefinger. My dad was looking at me. I was waiting for him to say, "You little bastard, stop that." But he didn't say that. He said, "Hey, roll me a bust of Lincoln, will you?" We laughed and laughed. You know, he did those kinds of things to me. I'll never forget it, and I told my own kid that, and he laughed like crazy. Humor has a way of lightening the load, and I'm finding that it is becoming more and more important to me as I grow older.

I don't mind that the time goes by. As I said, you got to check out some time; you can't stay here forever. You see a lot of people you know go. Well, you just hope you go with a little dignity, that you don't have to suffer from Alzheimer's or die slowly in a rest home alone somewhere. I thought it was very interesting when I was in Bora Bora for six months. I was down there making a movie, and Bora Bora is a place where they still have some of the old traditions of the natives. I did not live with the company, but found a house by myself up a road. There was a family next door—Polynesian natives—and the old lady of the house was there and she was dying. She suddenly said, "I'm going to die," and went to bed for three days and died. I remember at her funeral that everybody was dressed in white; it was like a wedding almost. And I was talking to them about it and they said, "Oh, yes, the fathers and the mothers are the most respected. They just go and die when they're ready." I said, "Geez, does that really go on like this all the time?" They said, "That's the way this society works." There are no old age homes, no old people wandering around, you know, suffering to death. Isn't it a strange thing, I thought to myself. What a respect for age that we don't have. And I thought, I wonder if we ever had that in this country, if back 100 years ago the frontiersmen treated the elderly with respect. What about Lincoln's family? Like I say, life is like a hotel. We all check in and we all check out. Seems to me that the Polynesian approach to checking out is a great deal better than ours.

Cesar Romero

▷   ▷   ▷   ▷   ▷   ▷   ▷   ▷   ▷

One of America's best known character actors, Cesar Romero has had a long and glorious career in film and television. His many film appearances include Wee Willie Winkie, Hot Millions, *and* Marriage on the Rocks. *He also appeared regularly on television in "Fantasy Island," "Batman," and "Charlie's Angels." Most recently he was a series regular on "Falcon Crest." He is eighty-five years old.*

I was never a leading man. I guess it's too late now.
[Laughs.] I was a character actor in most of the things
that I did. I played all kinds of characters, from Cortez
in *Captain from Castille* to the Joker in "Batman," so my
career has been a varied one. I've never been a straight
romantic leading man. Far and few between were the
pictures where I ended up with the girl. What can I say?

Today I'm very fortunate because I am still wanted
from time to time in Hollywood, which isn't the case for
most older actors. I work because I like to work. I like
to be busy in this industry because I love it. I started
back in 1926, you know, in New York, so I've been at
it for a long time. I don't know what I'd do with myself
if I didn't work. I don't work all the time, but it's
enough to satisfy me and enough to take care of my
needs. I'm very fortunate in that I don't have to work,
but I can because I like it—and because I'm still wanted.
I'm not as much in demand as I used to be—I'm not the
popular actor that I was years ago—and I see people
doing parts that I think I could have done or would have
liked to have done. But I've never had any doors slam
in my face. Most older actors are ignored completely,
but it hasn't happened to me yet.

I've been very fortunate that I haven't had to worry
about what's going to happen in my old age. I have
money and I still have work that I love. But for many
people, and I must include myself at times, it's not all
that beautiful getting old. No, I don't think it's the
greatest thing in the world. Getting old is a big pain,
really, but there's nothing I can do about it. I happen to

be lucky because I'm in good health, I'm active in my work, and I have a rich social life. Still, I don't enjoy getting old.

I'm going to be eighty-five in two months. I don't think I look eighty-five, I don't feel eighty-five, and I don't act like eighty-five. I have friends that are twenty years younger than I that look older and act older than I do. So I'm very fortunate in that respect. But a lot of it is luck. I don't blame my friends for looking older. As far as your appearance goes, I think your genes have a lot to do with it. My parents were young looking up to the day they died. I have my aches and pains; as you get older you can't help that. I have a slight amount of arthritis, but I don't let it get to me. And I've had back problems, but I do exercises to keep fit. Still, I'm convinced that a lot of it is in the genes.

The worst thing about growing old for me has been losing my close friends. All my old really intimate friends, my really very close friends, have passed away. People like Tyrone Power, Walter Lang, Gary Cooper —they're all gone. I do know many, many people, and I have a wonderful relationship with them, but they're not the kind of friends that I can call up and say, "I'm coming over to have a cup of coffee with you," or just stop in without being announced. I don't have that anymore. I miss it greatly.

When I think about it, it has been family that has been most important to me in life. I look back now and I'm thankful that I was able to care for my father (who had Parkinson's disease) and my mother and my grandmother. And now my sister lives with me. My family ties really kept me out of trouble, you know.

I tell you, I see some of the younger people today and it's very discouraging. They have no sense of values and so little respect for family traditions. You go down Sunset Boulevard at night and what you see is just frightening. It's frightening to see the young people that are just standing in the streets, the girls with their skirts way up to here. This is the youth of our country! I say to myself. If this is youth, give me old age. Years ago a family was mother, father, children, grandmother, grandfather, aunt, and uncle—that was a family. Today children are lucky if they have one parent. They don't have that family background. In many ways, my family was my life.

I was brought up in New York City. My father was the president of an exporting house on Wall Street called Augus and Fuller and Company. He exported sugar machinery and hardware to plantations in Cuba. I had all the best. I graduated from the oldest prep school in the country. But in 1922 the sugar market crashed, and it took my father with him. He lost everything. From that time on my parents had a rough time of it, and ever since then I decided that my first obligation was to assist my family because my parents were awfully good to me and to my sisters and to my younger brother. My father was completely defeated, completely, and many doctors said that could have caused his Parkinson's disease.

Taking care of my family became my greatest motivation in life. I don't know what it would have been like for me if I hadn't had that. I like to have fun and go out and have a good time, but I knew that I had to take care of my family. And sometimes I think that the reason I still have my health and my work at the age of eighty-five is that my family responsibility kept me out of trouble. Because, you know, as soon as I was on my feet out here in Hollywood I brought the whole family out here, brought them all out from New York. I bought a huge house and we all lived here together in Hollywood. And I've never regretted it; I was always thankful that I was able to do it.

I don't know what to tell you but that I feel that I'm a very fortunate man. Life has been good to me. I've had friends of mine that have had very troubled lives, but I've been very fortunate. Everybody should be as lucky as I have been. My secret to aging is just to be mindful of how fortunate you are. Count your blessings.

 Bruce Conklin

May Sarton

⫸　　⫸　　⫸　　⫸　　⫸　　⫸　　⫸　　⫸　　⫸

Born in Belgium, May Sarton came to the United States with her parents when she was two. Throughout her adolescence her vision of the world was accented by long visits and schooling in Europe. Although her father was a professor at Harvard University, she chose not to continue a formal education after graduating from high school.

May Sarton's published works have been contributing to American literature for more than fifty years. Her many volumes of poetry, her novels, and her personal journals depict her own struggles and relationships. Today, at the age

233

of seventy-five, she works and lives by herself in York, Maine, in a house by the sea.

But at seventy-four, May Sarton had a stroke. Although it was mild, she also suffered from a fibrillating heart condition that was difficult for her doctors to treat. In the nine months that followed until proper medications were regulated, the life she had carefully planned for herself was disrupted, and her view of the world changed as her own needs changed. The result of her recovery is evident in After the Stroke, *her latest journal.*

G rowing old is, I think, a very interesting process in which you begin to learn to give things up and to hang on to the most important things in your life. But when you're sick, as sick as I was, everything is taken from you at once. I jumped, I leaped into old age suddenly, without having a nice, slow preparation. Now I'm back again to where I was before, so I don't feel that old at all.

In a way, my sickness gave me a terrifying idea of what it might be like to be old when you are too ill to do anything, or if you have no family and you're not rich. But it's been wonderful to come back. The great advantage of going through something awful is, of course, that just the ordinary things become so precious. The fact that I can garden again is just heaven; well, that I can enjoy life again. And that I dare to have a little puppy. You know, everyone said, "Don't do that. You're too old." I said, "I have to have a puppy; I have to have someone who sleeps with me.'' You see, my dear Tamas, a Shetland collie, died at sixteen. I just adored him and I miss him every day. And I miss Bramble, my cat; they both died in that hard year of the stroke. It's like the break-up of a family. But now I have a little family again.

In some ways, I'm actually glad to be old. I have solved so many of the problems that are agonizing to the young, like the sexual problems. You've come to terms with your life and therefore it's much easier to lead it than when you're nineteen and you don't know who you are or what you want. I mean, I was in love with men and women, and it took me a long time to sort it all out. I just loved people. I had many love affairs; sometimes I look back on my life and think how shocked some people would be if they knew how many love affairs I had. But I've written about, I've shared these things with others, because I want to be open. ''Transparent'' is one of the words that comes through in all my work, and ''vulnerable.'' If you can't let pain in, you see, you'll never know joy. You really won't. You may be happy, but you'll never know joy.

It's poetry that means the most to me, but the work of my life is answering mail! And it never gets solved. There's no solution to that. I mean, one of the choices I would like to make is to not answer anymore, but I have many, many friends. You see, I'm seventy-five and I've accumulated people for seventy-five years. So when somebody writes and says, ''My mother is dying of cancer. I haven't communicated with you for so long, but I wanted you to know this. It's so hard,'' am I to say,

"I'm sorry, but I'm not answering letters anymore"?
No. If it's a friend, I answer. The people I now answer
less are the fans. I wish I could answer, because I want
to. I think there are about 400 letters unanswered up-
stairs in my study. Darling people writing, and you want
to do so much more than you can. At the same time,
you've got to learn that you can't and somehow take it
without too much frustration. That's the great lesson of
old age: to learn to say, "It's all right. You can't do it.
Do what you can."

I'm an avid gardener, you know; I couldn't live without flowers. Even when I was very poor I used to always
have one rose or something, a bunch of daisies, in my
room wherever I was. Flowers are so beautiful; they're
a tremendous aesthetic pleasure. And flowers have the
whole sequence of life in them, from the bud to death
and then growth again—everything about growth is in
the flower. In a way, it's all about life; each day has this
cycle for me. I mean, I wake up young and I go to bed
old. But it's a rich life. When I get very upset and
badgered by various things, I think, well, how would
you change it? And I realize that I'm living the life I've
chosen and I love my life—especially because I can
garden again. I'm Taurus, you see, the earth. Not having
been able to dig in the earth last year was very hard for
me psychologically. I lost something—some strength,
psychic strength—because I wasn't close to the earth
anymore.

Now I can live my ideal day once more. I get up at
five with the animals, let them out, and feed them. I
make my breakfast, take it up to bed, then spend an hour

where I try to really think out what I want to do with
the day; it's sort of a meditation. Then I get up and I'm
very busy for an hour, just washing dishes, making the
bed, watering the plants. About eight is my ideal time
to get to my desk. I don't work more than three hours
a day; that's all Virginia Woolf ever did. Three hours of
intense work is a lot. At eleven o'clock or so I get the
mail and have a drink of sherry because I'm very tired
by then—I've been up since five, you see. Then all of
life comes crashing in on me; somebody's in need,
somebody's dying, somebody needs money. All that's
buzzing around in my head. Then I have my lunch and
rest for an hour and a half. At three I get up and it's a
whole different day. I put on my gardening clothes
before I rest, because it's such an effort to change; if I'm
already dressed, I go out happily at three and garden for
two hours and a half. Then I come in and have a bath,
and then I have to get my dinner. And this is hard,
because I'm very tired from the physical work. Then I
go to bed at eight and read. The little dog is very anxious
to get to bed too, and the cat, so we all go up to sleep.
As long as one can maintain at least the structure of
one's life, then what goes on within it does change. You
have the form and you can fill it here or there, or not
fill it. Some days you can say, "I am just not going to
work today." But the structure is still there. I go up to
my desk every day, whether I work there or not. Sometimes I just sit there and think—not often, but I do.

I suppose my whole life could be defined as an acute
conflict between art and life, between what art asks and
what life asks. The conflict is what keeps you alive. It

would be a very dull life if I just did nothing but write up in that study and never saw a person. On the other hand, it would be an impossible life if I saw people all day. So it's a good balance. I wish I had a little more physical strength now, and didn't get so tired, but that's my age. You see, I can't quite accept yet that I'm seventy-five; it seems I don't feel that I'm seventy-five. But the fact is that I am. The diminution of energy is really the only thing that is hard to work with. But I feel happier now than I've ever been because I have served whatever small talent I have as well as I could.

Gretchen Stewart

Arthur Schlesinger, Jr.

❯   ❯   ❯   ❯   ❯   ❯   ❯   ❯   ❯

Arthur M. Schlesinger, Jr., won a Pulitzer in history in 1946 for The Age of Jackson *and a Pulitzer in biography in 1966 for* A Thousand Days: J.F.K. in the White House. *He is the Albert Schweitzer Professor in Humanities at the City University of New York. A graduate of Harvard, Schlesinger also studied at Peterhouse, Cambridge, and has been a professor of history at Harvard.*

I never feel seventy-four. I feel about forty most of the time and ninety part of the time, but never seventy-four. I feel fine. I play better tennis today than I did twenty years ago, so age thus far has been okay. Of course, when I was young, seventy was much older than it is today. When I was thirty in 1947, people were quite old at seventy-five. Now my contemporaries don't look to me as if they have changed much in the last twenty years. For whatever reason, people are younger today. You know how old Franklin Roosevelt was when he died? It was a month after his sixty-third birthday, and now we have presidents who are in their seventies.

I am sure that I am slowing up in various ways, but I don't detect any particular slackening of energy. If anything, I am busier than ever. One of the great illusions of life is that age brings simplification. In many cases—certainly in my case—age simply means that obligations and commitments and involvements accumulate. I'm getting goddamn tired of it, to be honest. Correspondence alone is a pain in the ass. But when people write serious letters, asking serious questions, you owe them an answer.

I've gotten more resolute in recent years. I turn down more things, but there are still too many obligations. For example, old friends appear and ask you to do forewords for their books . . . one thing after another, and I'm not sufficiently ruthless to say no. I have practically cut out lecturing, except for irresistible fees, because what I want to do is write books. I've dissipated enough of my life on good causes. It is time for younger people to take those up.

I suppose that I've always gotten involved in too many things—a bad habit I've tried to discipline with imperfect success. My chief objective in life is to write books, but there are public issues that interest me, and there's the need to make money. I've still got two children (out of six) in college and law school, and academic salaries just don't sustain all that. One lives from day to day. Let's put it this way: I'm far, far from retired. I don't want to be tied down. I want to keep my time as flexible as possible in the hope that I can get some of my own work done. I like to keep the future as clean and open as possible.

In your seventies, time becomes the most precious of commodities. The thing I resent most is wasting it. Up until the age of seventy time seems infinite, but time is now finite. Every once in a while when you go to a boring meeting or dinner party you wonder what in the hell you are doing wasting your time. I try and repent and swear not to get myself in that kind of situation again. Certain things I just don't do anymore. For example, I never go to lectures unless I'm giving them myself. [Laughs.] A number of things you cut out.

I'm much struck by a man whom I liked very much, Averell Harriman. He died at the age of ninety-four, but he retained his vigor well into his nineties. I think one great reason for it was that he had young friends. All through the forty years I knew him, he sought out young people as friends. That was partly an expression of his own youthfulness, but it certainly kept him in touch with everything and kept him young. I have youngish children, and I think that keeps one young.

Besides, I'm a historian. Historians tend, like musical conductors, to live to a ripe age and work to the end.

There was an American historian in the early part of the nineteenth century named George Bancroft, to whom I am related. Bancroft died at ninety-one, and there's a letter in which he describes a typical working day at the age of eighty-five. He worked for fourteen hours straight, only pausing to have a glass of water and a sandwich at lunch. My father was a historian and he died relatively young—at seventy-seven—but he worked up till the day he died. Historians are lucky that way. Curiosity is our bedmate, so we are never satisfied. We are always trying to discover new things, finding out about things, and keeping at it, staying the course.

I think my primary desire now is to finish up my book projects. Many years ago I embarked on a study of the Roosevelt presidency called *The Age of Roosevelt*. Three volumes have already come out, and finishing up that series is my initial objective. I suppose someday I may do a memoir of some sort. But, for the moment, life moves from engagement to engagement, in spite of my efforts at simplification. Perhaps in a year or so I'll have learned how to say no. Check back.

Roddy McDowall

Charles Schulz

⪼   ⪼   ⪼   ⪼   ⪼   ⪼   ⪼   ⪼   ⪼

The creator of "Peanuts"—The Charlie Brown Gang—is a tall, handsome, mild mannered seventy-year-old gentleman who speaks softly with a flat, Midwestern accent. His crew-cut hairstyle from youthful days has given way to a more conventional style and his hair is now a silvery grey. His warm, loveable puppy Snoopy is probably the most famous dog in the world. The forty-one-year-old comic strip "Peanuts" appears in more than 2,000 newspapers every day and is read by an estimated 100 million people. Schulz's creative *vision is better known around the world than Rembrandt's, yet his conversation reflects gratitude and modesty.*

I've been very fortunate, very fortunate. Fabulous things have happened to me—more than I ever expected. I'm getting older, yet I continue to produce good material, although I'm ever mindful of the dangers of growing dull. I suppose from a commercial or a business standpoint, one of the most delightful experiences for me was standing in the theater lobby of the Little Fox Theater in San Francisco when *You're a Good Man, Charlie Brown* was being performed, and seeing the family groups come out with everyone smiling and knowing that they had really seen something that was delightful and nice and totally harmless, not offensive in any way, proving that it can be done. I always thought that that was great. And I've had a lot of other personal triumphs. Having a one-man show at the Louvre last year and receiving the Order of the Commander of Arts and Letters from the minister of culture, Jack Lang, was a tremendous experience, something that I never even dreamed of having happen. To have your cartoons hang in an exhibit in the Louvre is just astounding for a young, unknown kid from St. Paul, Minnesota.

I do think about growing old all the time. I worry about it, you know. When I had bypass surgery, which has been just about ten years ago now, I dreaded it. I'd never come close to an experience like that. The thought of having one's chest sawed open is extremely frightening. But I had great confidence in the surgeon once I got to know him and I kept thinking, If I can go through this and survive it, it will be a great accomplishment; it will be like having come out of the war and having survived it and having done your duty. If I can survive this surgery it will be a tremendous accomplishment and I'll feel real good about myself when it's all done. I will be very grateful for the years that have been given to me. But I discovered that human beings are not made that way. You quickly forget and soon become what you always were. I'm pretty convinced that this is the way we are made. If we are normal people, we don't remember all the bad things; we just remember the good things. I think this is what has helped mankind to survive all of these thousands of years.

The white hair part of growing old doesn't bother me. I began to turn gray in my twenties, so that has never really bothered me. The wrinkles also don't bother me because I think a lot of them are smile wrinkles, which I think is something to be grateful for. I have one eyelid that has become slightly droopy, and I know that doctors can repair that sort of thing these days, but I don't want to go through that. It dismays me sometimes when I think that I'm looking real good and then look in the mirror when I might be talking to somebody and discover that I look just terrible. And, of course, if you're at all athletic, and I've been reasonably athletic throughout my life—I play golf, tennis, and I still play ice hockey—it is disappointing to see that you are not as fast or as strong as you used to be. This is a slight cause for despair. I do not have the wind to take part in some sports that I had when I was in the infantry, when I could have run forever. But, after all, I've had a quadruple bypass and I've also had knee surgery from a hockey injury, so that has a little bit to do with it. I realize that this is just the way things happened, so I certainly don't complain about it. I'm not the greatest senior hockey player in the world, but I'm also not the worst, so that makes me feel all right.

One of the worst parts about growing old is the feeling that I've had recently of a winding down experience. When you're gathered around with your family, at Christmas for instance, the thought occurs to you, Is this going to be my last Christmas? When you see your grandchildren, you recognize that you probably will never be around to see them graduate from high school or go to college. This is sad, but these are things over which we have no control. Take your own life and what is happening to you, and then look at the lives of friends that you've lost and all the people who died at a younger age than you are now. It makes you realize that you are very fortunate to have whatever health you have now; you are fortunate to just be here. I know there are some people who never even think about these things, but this is one of the curses of a vivid imagination, and whatever success I've had has been the result of that vivid imagination. Fortunately, it's an imagination that also produces funny responses, which helps me cope with a memory that dredges up all sorts of sad things in life.

Like all old people I am appalled at the way time goes by, that before I know it it's time to start sending out Christmas cards again. I am dismayed at the way my months and years are planned and taken away from me before they even begin. If I can survive this year, I want to make sure that next year is not all taken up already with scheduled events. I just can't stand that sort of life where I have obligations continually, every week and every month. I find myself almost without a perfectly clear, clean, pure five-day week ahead of me where I can just simply do my work and not have any obligations. It just doesn't happen anymore.

I just want to do what I want to do for a change. Somebody said, "Well, what is it you want to do?" And I said, "Nothing. I just want to stay home with my dog." I do have many evenings where I can go home and just do nothing. I just sit in my big chair and I have my little TV clicker and I run up and down the channels and shoot from one thing to another. My dog jumps up on the hassock in front of me and asks for another cookie and I give it to him and he jumps down and I click from one program to another, and then he jumps up on the hassock and he wants another cookie and I give him another doggie cookie and he jumps down again—and that's our life. Pretty soon it's 9:30 and it's time to go to bed.

I'm great for doing nothing. I remember years ago when my son Craig was small and he was talking about what we all did, and somebody said, "Well, what do you do, Craig?" He said, "I don't do anything, I just hang around." It's almost something that has to be learned, and I don't see anything wrong with it. I think that learning to just hang around is all right; just to be able to sit in a chair and stare into space. I'm not adverse at all, if I have to meet somebody, to be a half hour early just standing on the corner or sitting in the hotel lobby doing nothing. I don't feel that I have to be reading something or writing something or being continually active. I don't mind hanging around.

I believe that a comic strip artist should get better the older he gets, as long as he remains healthy. Mechanically I have a slight problem in that my hand is not as steady as it was back in the middle twenties when I first started drawing seriously. I used to pride myself on having a good pen line, and so this caused me a slight bit of despair several years ago, but now I've learned to live with it. I simply prop one hand against the other and I don't try for the effects that I might have tried for when I was younger and had a steady hand. I think the big danger with a cartoonist or a comic strip artist growing older is that he runs the danger of becoming a boring person. And if you are boring yourself (and a lot of old people are boring), then the things that you create will be boring too. This could very well happen. It's one of the few things that I worry about.

Something else that is much more profound is that you could run out of life experiences, which is what makes you boring. If you cease to become interested in people around you, if you cease to do any productive reading, listening, looking, watching, and all of that, then you will have used up all of the experiences of your life and will begin to draw upon your capital. F. Scott Fitzgerald used to worry about becoming emotionally bankrupt, and I think you could become bankrupt in this manner. I don't think it has happened to me as yet, although there are days when I get scared. Sometimes I just sit and simply can't think of anything new because I've had no new experiences to draw upon; all of my old themes just seem to have been used up. It is possible, then, that you just end up drawing the same things all of the time. Now that is scary.

I think it takes maturity to learn how to be alone. One of the great accomplishments of maturity is learning to be with yourself, all alone. Anybody who says that he or she is bored is committing a terrible sin. We should never be bored in this wonderful world in which we live. You know, there's a million things to do every day, and to be bored is really a sin against our Creator because there are so many things to do, even if that's just loafing and enjoying it. It takes maturity to really make the most out of your days.

.

Pete Seeger

≫　　≫　　≫　　≫　　≫　　≫　　≫　　≫　　≫

Pete Seeger was one of the first young Yankee college students to fall in love with Southern folk music. Over forty-five years of concerts (many with his friend and colleague Woody Guthrie) he has managed to interest thousands in the idea of making their own music and reviving traditional music of many types. Blacklisted during the McCarthy years for refusing to bend to unwarranted accusations, Pete Seeger has used music to struggle against war, racism, poverty, and, more recently, environmental pollution. He is seventy years old and continues to maintain a full schedule of performances.

In sailing we have a saying: "There are old pilots and there are bold pilots, but there are no old, bold pilots." So I think one should praise old people because they managed to get old. You don't manage to get old if you're too careless or reckless. And, you know the old joke: growing old is a lot better than the alternative.

When I reflect on where I am, I just feel blessed. I have good health and energy and a family that has stuck by me, even when they disagreed with me. And I have a large family. I lived with my grandparents as a child, and I had in-laws living near us when our children were small. Now I'm a grandfather in a three-generation household, and I have a lot of brothers and sisters and nephews and nieces. So I feel I'm just very lucky to have health and family. Also, I was able to make a living all my life doing something I loved. Think how many people have had to scramble just to pay the rent all their lives. My kids never went hungry. Oh, we pinched pennies, but that's the way things should be when you think of the people in this world who don't have a penny to their name—it's kind of immoral not to pinch pennies in a way.

I'm an old grandpa now. When I go out singing, I don't have much of a voice, but larger audiences than ever come to listen. I used to sing in Pittsburgh for a hundred people here, or two hundred there, but Arlo Guthrie and I went back and sang for 50,000 in a local park. So there are advantages to being a grandpa.

Another advantage is that you gain a bit of insight, a little more wisdom. That's one of the by-products of living a long time. I do know that I am more suspicious than ever, though, about words. We used to have a little sign hung up on this sloop club here where we're talking and it said, "In trying to persuade others, setting a good example is not the best thing; it is the only thing." And it's signed "Albert Schweitzer." There's an old Southern saying, "I wish his 'do so' would match his 'say so.'" But, you know, I don't do as good a job of it as I wish I could. I still talk too much and don't act enough. Somebody, I don't know who, said, "Words lie halfway between thought and action, and too often substitute for both."

I guess I've gradually come to the opinion that everything's connected more closely than I realized. You can't really solve the problem of poverty on earth unless you can also solve the problem of pollution on earth. And vice versa. My guess is we won't solve the problem of racism and sexism and a whole lot of other things until each of us, individually, realizes how much we depend on others—sometimes those near and dear to us, sometimes those faraway and unknown. It gets you to thinking about eternity, about the spiritual, about the ways we are connected to one another.

These days, I look upon God as everything. Some people say, "Oh, God is in everything." Well, that's our difference of opinion. If I was able enough to look through an electron microscope, to see something one-millionth of an inch in size, they'd say, "That's God's handiwork." But I'd say, "That *is* God." If I was able to look at the screens of a radar telescope to see something five billion light years away, I'd be looking at God there too. They say, "Well, that's the handiwork of God." Well, okay, that's our difference of opinion. And consider that five billion miles away is a long ways, but it's nothing compared to infinity. I really believe that God is infinite.

The late great mathematician and philosopher Alfred North Whitehead said that religion is the ideal of education throughout the ages because it inculcates duty and reverence. I think that's a good definition of religion— duty and reverence. He says, "Duty arises from our potential control over the course of events, and reverence arises from the perception that the present includes the complete sum of existence, that great amplitude of time, forward and backward, which is eternity." If that can't make you reverent, I don't know what would. We live in a web of interconnections. If I slap my hands together and I disturb some atoms, they're going to disturb other atoms and they're going to push others and, in effect, have influence for all eternity to come. That can make you reverent.

I try very hard to see the world as a whole, and I try to remind myself as much as possible that you can accomplish more with good deeds than bad deeds. The USA would like to have influence throughout the world, but we could have far more influence throughout the world right now if we had not spent three trillion dollars or more on guns and bombs in the last few decades. And they have plans for spending another trillion in the next few years with fancy, new, high-tech weapons in the sky and so on. But we wouldn't have needed any of these high-tech weapons if we'd spent half that amount of money on schools and colleges and training institutions throughout the entire world, because how are the billions of people in the world going to get out from behind the eight ball? True, they need food, but food is a temporary thing, as you know. Remember the old Chinese saying, "Give a man a fish, you can feed him, but teach him how to fish and he'll feed himself a long time." And so, if there was one wish I could have, I guess it would be for the world to learn this lesson, which it seems it still hasn't learned yet. The leaders of the world are saying, "Well, the way we solve this problem is to get rid of those people." That's their solution. But Abe Lincoln said it much better: "It's good to get rid of an enemy, but the best way to get rid of the enemy is to make him your friend." The important thing is, of course, the long human chain we are a part of; if we don't do right, this chain's going to be broken in too many places. The world may keep on turning, but it may not have any human beings on it, or maybe not any life at all. I think we have to face up to this possibility.

Growing up is about becoming responsible, about lending ourselves and our talents and our energies to the great chain that connects us all. Ronnie Gilbert sings a wonderful song called "Activities Room," and it's a series of short dialogues in an old-age home. It starts off with a woman trying to persuade another woman to join the bridge club. She says, "Oh, I've forgotten how to play." She finally gives up and says, "OK, I'll join the club." And then it has another person trying to persuade somebody to join the billiard tournament. And he says,

"Oh, I haven't played billiards for so long I don't think I can still do it." But he ends up deciding to join. And the last verse is about somebody who's asked to join the orchestra. And he says, "Oh, my lips are all out of shape; I haven't played horn in years. Maybe I could get 'em back in shape; I'll try." So this is, of course, the world's best advice to any old person: You don't give up simply because you're not as good at it as you might have been; you still have fun with it. And this goes for almost anything. You do have to recognize limitations, or else you literally won't live long. Don't try and repeat your successes of youth; the aim is to have fun. And within your limitations you *can* have a lot of fun.

It's often good, as we know, to get together with others of the same age, and quite often I sing for senior citizens groups around my hometown here. I also advise them, though, to be of help and to volunteer at jobs that they are often better at than younger people—taking care of kids, for example. It's true you don't have the energy to take care of huge numbers of kids, but there are often people who say, "If I could only find someone to help watch my kids while I go shopping or while I'm at work." They just need a dependable person who will see that their child is not getting hurt. I think people who live a long time do somehow learn patience, and they can teach little children patience also. Volunteering to help with young people is one of the most wonderful things. I have some friends who have enriched their own lives by being a part of a program called Foster Grand-parents. They don't have any of their own grandchildren handy, so they are grandparents to somebody else's.

I myself stay active doing a wide variety of things, some intellectual, others physical. I do an average of about three hours a week working in the woods around my house, because we burn four or five cords of stove wood every year. It's good exercise and kind of nice to be out in the woods, listening to the birds and seeing the leaves and the beauties of nature. It's also a time to reflect. In many ways those are the most satisfactory hours of my week. I get away from the telephone and just get to think. In fact, more often than not the ideas I get for music or songs will come during those hours because in the day there's just too many things going on.

I'm just an old do-it-yourselfer, you know. I think there is a limit to specialization, and I take great pleasure in learning how to do new things. Now, there are times, I'll admit, when I'll be glad to let somebody else do things for me. I was very glad to have an expert doctor repair my knee when I foolishly tore the ligament in it; otherwise, I'd have been on crutches the rest of my life. But by and large, I love to see people in the world trying to do more things and not just watching other experts do it. My father put it in a good way: "Judge the musicality of a nation not by the presence of virtuosos, but by the general level of people who like to make music." It's kind of the equivalent of what W. E. B. Du Bois, the great black scholar, said: "I'd count the wealth of a nation not by the presence of millionaires, but by the absence of poverty."

My father told me there was a graveyard in Tombstone, Arizona, with a little wooden cross over some cowboy's grave and somebody had scrawled on it, "He done his damnedest.'' And really, that's all we can do in this world: We do our best wherever we are to be a strong link in the chain. If we can be a strong link, we should know how lucky we are, even though the links to come never knew our name, don't know where or when we lived. But in the future, assuming there is a future, they'll know that they would not be there if it hadn't been for a lot of links that came before. I tell my grandson, ''Now, there's a whole lot of ancestors you've got—they're scattered all around the world, and I don't know their names—but I know one thing: not one of them died childless.''

Artie Shaw

≫ ≫ ≫ ≫ ≫ ≫ ≫ ≫ ≫

Multitalented Artie Shaw has spent a lifetime engaged in creative pursuits, from songwriting to filmmaking, music making to book writing. From 1936 through 1954 he was the leader of the Artie Shaw Band, which won the Downbeat Award as the best American swing band and the Esquire Magazine Award as the favorite band of the armed services. In more recent years Artie Shaw has turned his attention to writing. He is the author of The Trouble with Cinderella, I Love You, I Hate You, Drop Dead, *and* The Best of Intentions and Other Stories. *In 1986 a film about his life,* Artie Shaw: Time Is All You've Got, *won an Academy Award as the best feature-length documentary.*

Eighty-one years old, Artie Shaw makes his home in Newbury Park, California. His study, where this interview took place, is jammed with books on nearly every conceivable subject.

Well, when you're in this room, you're walking around inside my head. These are the things that form my mind. I've got books here that I haven't looked at for forty-five years, but whenever I need something, instead of having to go to a library and asking a reference librarian, here it is. This is me, this is my brain. An awful lot of what I know in terms of Culture, capital C, is here.

I'm not an especially happy man, but I'm not a sad one either. Happiness, as I've written, is not a state like Rhode Island that you drive into. I don't know what happiness means. I know I feel good, I'm fairly content, I like what I do, I like my life, but what is there to be happy about, if you look around? You'd have to be a dope to be happy. If I consider where I live and I look at Lithuania, though, I'm pretty lucky. If I look at this as the ideal state, then it's miserable.

It's a stupid country we live in. Democracy is one of the worst systems on earth, but we've got nothing better. People say what about democracy? "Great idea, let's try it." Civilization the same. "Civilization, it's a nice idea, we really ought to try it." Actually this civilization of ours is a bit depressing. I was talking with some woman not long ago, and I said to her, "Can you imagine anybody fifty years from now saying, 'I want the collected works of Boy George'?" She said, "Well, you can't knock him, he's doing pretty well." I said, "What are you talking about? If he wants to do well, why doesn't he get into real estate or banking? Why make rotten music?" I look at the freeway and I'm amazed that they don't kill each other with the stupidity that's all over the place, with the total self-seeking "Screw you, I've got mine" attitude that's engendered by our culture. I'm amazed that the freeway isn't a long line of mangled wreckage and corpses. I'm astounded that the whole culture works. What really astounds me is that people can live their whole lives and not learn one goddamn thing. That is one of the most amazing facts I know. Most people are caught up in absurd pursuits— How much money can I make and how big a house and how expensive a car can I drive?

Time triggers everything, and it's taken me many, many years to realize that time should not be trivialized; it should be used. It's the only thing we have. It should not be used to see how much money you can make, or how much influence or power you can gain, but what you can do with it to better the world. How can you live a semi-artistic life in a totally materialistic world? That is the question. My gag with people is, "If you're so smart, why aren't you poor?" Most people go the other way; they think smart means money. Smart doesn't mean money, and wise doesn't mean money. Anyway, I'm cursed with the need to investigate the basic phenomena of the world, including Who am I?, Why am I here?, What am I doing?, How long will I be here?, What's the purpose of anything?, and Is there a purpose? All of those questions—you know, the big ones: Who are we? Where did we come from? Where do we go?

After teaching a course once, I wound up by asking my class this question: "All right, we've been yammering at each other for three weeks now, and I've brought up a number of profound questions to which I know there are no answers. What do you get out of all this?" And one old man said a neat thing: "You seem to be saying we pass this way but once, so pay attention." That is the point; I've learned to pay attention. Mostly you get on a plane and you fly to New York. There's a continent going by, but you don't pay attention. Well, it used to take three months to make that passage. Now we do it in a matter of hours and we're impatient, because it's five hours, my God, five hours to cross the country. The point I'm making here is I've learned—finally—that the whole idea of piling up more, more, more on top of more, more, more is a rather fruitless occupation.

The old gag is, "If I can't take it with me, I won't go." Well, there's no question you've got to go, that's one undeniable fact. I mean, even taxes are not undeniable—you can get away with that—but death is going to get you. As W. C. Fields said, "The man in the bright nightgown will show up one day." Well, I'm prepared for him. If he shows up I'm going to say, "Look, I'm not ready yet, but if you insist, I'll go." It can't be ignored that we are finite, but I can't conceive of myself not *being*, so I don't think about it too often.

About the word talent: My view is, the person who has talent and acts as if he hasn't and works as hard as if he doesn't, that's the one who's got a chance at building something of world importance. Otherwise you're another tinkerer, and there's nothing wrong with that either, if it satisfies you. Anyway, death is like that. The person who lives as if there is no death has got a chance of doing something with the life that he has. If you constantly think about death, you become a religious freak or some weird character. I have no time for that.

Somebody called me the other day and he was very disappointed in something and he said, "I think I'll kill myself." And I said, "What's your hurry?" And he started to laugh. And, you know, what is the hurry? You don't have to kill yourself; it's being done for you. There are trillions of microbes out there plotting. "Let's get that sonofabitch," they're saying, "We'll get him, let's invade him." I mean, you're given this time to breathe, and we're trapped in this particular stratum we live in, so you might as well use it.

The only thing I care about, really, is learning and sensing and being part of the world I live in; seeing it and observing it and marveling at it. I'm trying to find out who I am; it's the endless puzzle. How did I get here? How did I get to this crazy place called the world? How did this phenomenon called "me" get here? I don't know. And when I look back at my life I absolutely marvel that I've got this far. I should have been expunged, I don't know how long ago. I must have been obnoxious because I was in such a hurry to get where I didn't even know I was going. You know, there's a great joke. A man's sitting in a barber chair and he's all swathed in towels—the barber's getting ready to shave him—and somebody runs in and says, "Jake, Jake, your house is on fire." The guys throws off the towels and runs down the street. After he's gone a block he says, "What am I running for? My name isn't Jake." Well, that was me. I sure was running, but I had no idea what the hell I was running for.

Simplify, simplify. That's what I'm working on these days. People are always saying, "Why don't you come visit?" Somebody called the other day and asked me to come visit them in Connecticut. My idea of a trip these days is one where I can be home by noon. You can't do anything worth doing if you don't simplify. The world is engaged in a monstrous conspiracy to stop you from doing what you should be doing. Another line I keep quoting is, "We can all do better than we do." But we don't because we divert ourselves—through movies, television, name it, one after another, baseball, sports—there's no end to it. Who's got time for all those trivialities?

It's to be hoped that as we grow older we mature—until we rot. I suppose I'm more mature now in the sense that I've had more time to think about the phenomena of existence. It comes down to this: "The more you know about everything, the more resonant what you do will be." It will ring. Everything that I know goes into my work, my life. As you get older, your sensibilities become more and more refined and what you do must benefit, or must in any case become more refined. So the more you know about everything, the better you will be at what you do, whatever that is.

I think many things are pretty absurd, and there's a sense of absurdity in everything I say, of course. I mean, we are really very puny creatures in the face of this enormous vastness out there. God, for example, at least as most people comprehend Him, is a silly notion. I got into a debate with a woman from the Canadian Broadcasting Corporation, a woman who was writing about females versus males. They asked me to come and debate her, and at one point she said, "Well, God says that women are superior, etc." I said, "When's the last time you talked to him?" And that stopped her dead, because I don't think anybody ever asked her that. It's a terrible presumption to talk about God as if you know what this enormous thing called infinity is.

I'm very alive, and I'm going to keep living until that man with the bright nightgown shows up. And then I'm going to argue with him. I'm not about to go gently into that dark night. No, that's a line I don't like; it's a sick joke that when we begin to know something about what life's about it's almost over. That's terrible, that's a sick rotten joke if I ever heard one. I'm constantly dealing with that absurdity. You say to yourself, Here I've learned all this stuff and now I'm supposed to die like that idiot down the street. And be just as dead as he is. That's the one point I cannot get my mind around. I can't make myself believe there is no purpose. I ask myself all the time, Why are you bothering? Why? Because something in me makes me, and whatever that is is as close to a definition of soul that I know of. I can't argue with that because it's operating, and as long as that keeps operating I have to believe there's some reason.

I don't know the answers, I just know I know a lot of questions. And I feel that the search for the answers to those questions is as good a way to spend your time as any I know of. I don't see how anybody can spend his life in this world and run out of things to do. Anybody who's bored is boring. How can you get bored?

Time is all we've got. I don't know what else we are given. *Who's Who* asked me for an epitaph. I think they do that when you get to be seventy-five or so. So I gave them an epitaph at seventy-five: "He did the best he could with the material at hand." Recently they asked me for an update, so it'll be, "Or, the abbreviated version: Go Away." That's my new epitaph. I mean, what else is there to say when you're lying there? I can't see any reason to get solemn about this. I find it fascinating, I find it funny, but mainly I find it very, very interesting to keep looking around and marveling at everything that goes on. We're here to search; we pass this way but once, so pay attention. That's it. Somebody once said, "I don't know if there's a hereafter, but I might as well gamble that there is." What other choice do we have? It's the only crap game in town, you know.

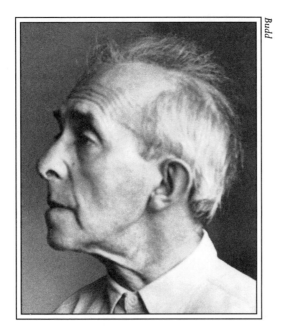

Budd

Raphael Soyer

⋙   ⋙   ⋙   ⋙   ⋙   ⋙   ⋙   ⋙   ⋙

Until his death in 1989, eighty-seven-year-old Raphael Soyer still attended to his daily business—painting. What he painted were the people, activities, and scenes of his adopted city, New York. He lived with his wife, Rebecca, in the heart of Manhattan, and maintained his studio in an old building on the Upper West Side. His workspace was sparse, unadorned. It was a simple room with an easel that had accompanied him on all of his moves. The walls had canvas tacked onto them, and there were brushes and paint tubes, but little else. Known as one of America's leading realist

*painters, Raphael Soyer had exhibited all his life. Presently,
the largest body of his work is in the permanent collection of
the Hirshhorn Museum in Washington, D.C.*

*Raphael Soyer was born one week before the beginning of
the twentieth century. His family left Russia in 1912 and
settled in New York City. He began to earn his place in art
history during the 1920s in a movement labeled American
Realism, where he was among a number of artists involved
in what they called "a conscious rediscovery of America."
These artists painted with a drastic realism that exposed what
they saw as the vacancy and frustration of American urban
and rural life. American Realism turned out to be more than
a phase for Raphael Soyer—it became his language.*

A s I have grown older I have begun more and more
to appreciate youth. You see, when you get old
you gain something, but you lose something very important. For instance, I remember when I was young that
every new painting to me was like a discovery. And my
early work had a certain poetic quality, something that's
a combination of innocence and instinctive wisdom.
That innocence you lose as you get older. You gain
wisdom, you become stronger in your judgments, but
you lose innocence—or at least I have. I have become
more flamboyant as I have aged. My work is more
colorful and my compositions more complicated, but I
have lost the very beautiful quality that young people
have. When I look at some of my earlier paintings, some
that I still like, I see something very beautiful there. I

don't try to recapture those qualities, because I can't. It's useless to try. You can't return to childhood.

I hate to admit it, but I believe in youth rather than age. I think that young people outstrip older people very easily. I like young people. They are bright, they are intelligent, they are full of excitement. Most older people bore me.

At one time I thought that to outlive my contemporaries would be a kind of triumph, but now I become very sad because most of my friends are gone—actually, all of my friends are gone. I have no people to talk to. I used to speak Russian with my brother all the time—I love the Russian language—but now I have no one to speak Russian with. So it is lonely. It makes me very melancholy. I miss these people. And missing them reminds me that I too will be leaving the stage sometime soon. There are moments when I don't know how many pluses there are to living as long a life as I have.

I try not to complain too much, but I do from time to time. Please forgive me. The only thing that I'm lucky about is that I still have my work. Thank God I still have my work. Artists never retire. They work up to the very last minute, and I intend to do the same. If I stopped working, I would die very soon. I'm eighty-six, so I may not have much time left. I'm ready anytime. I have lived a long time, but I'm not going to stop until I'm taken away. I still find bliss in my work. The thing that brings me joy in these final days is coming to this studio.

Studs Terkel

≫   ≫   ≫   ≫   ≫   ≫   ≫   ≫   ≫

Studs Terkel's voice has become as familiar as a favorite piece of furniture to the listeners of his Chicago-based radio program, which is syndicated nationally. Each day he speaks with authors, social activists, singers, and musicians. Sometimes he reads short stories, plays records, or hosts a dramatic presentation. Studs is known for his celebration of the unknown hero—the common man, be it the traffic cop, the waitress, the metal welder, or the switchboard operator. He's written several best-selling oral histories, among them The

Good War, American Dreams Lost and Found, *and* Working.

W hen I think of truly creative old people, I think of Verdi. He wrote *Falstaff* when he was eighty, and it was perhaps his greatest opera. He did *Othello* when he was seventy-four. And then there's Picasso. Need we say anymore? Or Casals playing Bach, always finding new aspects of Bach. So I'm sure that age has nothing to do with limiting creativity. If anything, it may produce a mellower aspect to creative pursuits.

But aging hasn't made me too mellow. It may have done the opposite. [Laughs.] I'm the last angry man. It's just beginning for me. I think that I get angrier now more than I ever did. I'm furious. I'm less inhibited in old age about showing my anger at something. When Reagan was constantly insulting the intelligence of the American electorate and they were accepting it, it drove me nuts. So I feel today much like Murphy in *One Flew Over the Cuckoo's Nest.* Do you remember that movie? Jack Nicholson played Murphy. I feel more and more like Murphy. Am I surrounded by lobotomized people? Eventually Murphy gets lobotomized himself. I don't want to smash a window to let the fresh air in or to escape. I have a fantasy that I've done something— committed a terrible public nuisance—and they finally pin me down to the table like they did Murphy. And there's a big nurse looking down at me, and I look up and see the face of Jeanne Kirkpatrick and say: "This is it. What are you doing?'' And she says: ''Well, we've performed a little operation on you. It won't hurt you, because everybody has gone through it here. You just happened to have escaped our safety net. It's called a lobotomy, so don't worry about it.'' And I say: ''Well, that's it.'' So maybe that will be the ending. [Laughs.]

I'm not mellow. Lots of angry outbursts these days. I'm comfortable enough to express my anger publicly. Often. And maybe it's keeping me alive. I want to be involved in the world, to see it getting better. So I protest from time to time. If the airline attendants go on strike and they ask me to come out, I say sure. I did one recently for the United strikers. That's a part of my life. I'm not saying that it keeps you young, but it does. It keeps the juices flowing. I'm asked why I take part in these extracurricular things that I have done through the years—from the age of twenty-five some fifty years ago. Why? As a phrase that Dorothy Day, the Catholic worker, once used: ''I'm working toward a world in which it would be easier for people to behave decently.'' I'd settle for that. My little contributions keep the blood coursing.

I don't think of age, really, except now and then, in a somewhat physical sense. Aside from that, I always think of what will be the next book. What will it be? I'm asked by others: ''What will be your last book?'' And I say: ''Why? Unless I die unexpectedly or something, I don't feel any diminishing power.''

You see, I like to think of something Lotte Lehmann, a great singer of this century, once said. Luckily I heard her recording of her final concert at Town Hall; she says: "You know, this is my last concert." And you hear the audience hollering: "No!" "Yes, and let me tell you why." You see, she has celebrated her role as the Marschallin in Richard Strauss's *Rosenkavalier*. Now, the Marschallin is a beautiful woman—only in her thirties, you see. She has this young lover, about eighteen. And she looks in the mirror and sees her first wrinkle or the intimation of one. She's still a beautiful and attractive woman, but that's it, that's the sign. So she gives up her young lover to the young girl, Sophie, and she does this soliloquy about the oncoming. Lotte says in the farewell talk to her audience: "I learned from the role of the Marschallin. You don't know, but I know it. And I will still be doing work, I'll still be teaching, I'll still be painting." It was other work she wanted to do. And she became a great teacher. She says: "I know, not the audience. I have overstayed my welcome."

Lotte made her decision. And it is a decision all of us should make for ourselves. So I'm totally opposed to mandatory retirement, which would mean that right now I would have to retire, wouldn't it, if I was on the CBS network. That's nonsense. But if I was a welder at the Ford plant or GM, and each day for thirty years had a welding gun in my hand, not moving and shooting spots into a revolving snake on the assembly line—if I did that, I'm longing for retirement, waiting for it. That's why the United Auto Workers had thirty years and you're out. Well, that's different. That person wants to go fishing—my God, of course!—and to be taken care of. But mandatory retirement to a professor who is enjoying his class very much in literature or psychology is ridiculous. I know a couple of guys who died a year after they retired, distinguished professors who didn't want to go but were forced to. How can you tell Verdi when he reaches the age of eighty, "That's it!" Well, there'd be no *Falstaff.*

It is horribly obvious that there is ageism in our society. There are also these obscene commercials. One is an ad for a lotion to take away the "ugly age freckles"—that's the actual phrase they use! Aging is ugly to them, a disease like leprosy. And the other commercial is one in which they dye this guy's hair. The guy looked pretty good with gray hair. Now you've got the guy with black hair. To me that's directly part of the phoniness of that being. I suppose plastic surgery is all part of it. Age is being thought of as something to be avoided.

The secret is to remain vital, and the secret to that is becoming involved or interested in something outside yourself. You have a society in which the values daily are "I'm going to make it! I don't give a goddamn!" My God, the self-indulgence! It's exactly the opposite that will keep the vitality going. It's as simple as that.

So, vitality is important. Humor is too. Without a sense of humor, I don't see how one could actually survive a day without suffocating. Even the macabre humor, the dark humor is needed. Every now and then I'm bawled out by a listener on my radio program because I laugh at a moment when something terrible has happened. There was, for instance, a piece in *The New Yorker* about a girl called Sylvia who was in a mental institution. I thought it hilarious, or rather something that Sylvia did. And of course I got a furious letter:

"You'd laugh at a concentration camp or a crutch!" That's not it. It so happens that when somebody is disturbed, and that person is full of imagination, some of the things she says or does are hilarious. It could be scatalogical, it could be brilliant, it could be disoriented—but it's funny! It's a terrible dilemma being mentally ill, but it also has a built-in goofy humor to it. What makes Charlie Chaplin so great is precisely that. In a moment of wild drama or tragedy he'd do a very funny little thing. If I was to have a guide for living, it would be Charlie Chaplin.

Beatrice Wood

≫ ≫ ≫ ≫ ≫ ≫ ≫ ≫ ≫

W herever I am, the song of life goes on. In other words, I really am never bored. I think it's a blessing to be ninety, because you don't fuss anymore about what is right or wrong. So a great deal of energy is not wasted.

The infectious sparkle of the ceramic artist Beatrice Wood is immediately apparent. Age has neither diminished her clarity nor changed her attitude. Her independent feisty spirit has characterized both her lifestyle and her work. Her career as an artist began as an act of defiance. While still in her teens she left a comfortable and secure home to seek the bohemian life in Paris. Those years brought hard financial times. But Beatrice Wood's life was filled with stimulating people and interesting experiences. The artist Marcel Duchamp became her friend and encouraged her to continue drawing and sketching. She was accepted in the art circles of that time, and her spirited and humorous drawings gave her visibility and prestige.

For many years Beatrice Wood had a mobile lifestyle that provided travel between Paris, New York, and Los Angeles. Then, in the early 1930s, her first involvement with ceramics introduced her to the medium that would occupy her interests for the next fifty years. As ceramics and the discovery of new glazing techniques became a serious pursuit, she moved to a combined studio and living space in the peaceful Ojai Valley seventy miles north of Los Angeles, where to this day she actively continues to draw and write and diligently produce her widely acclaimed work.

I looked in the mirror the other morning and I said, "Oh, there's a horse. I look like a horse." Well, what of it? I do look like a horse. But then I have fun making up and combing my hair, and then it doesn't bother me anymore that I'm old. I can't tell you why.

I love being old. First of all, I don't think about it too often. If I want to do something, I don't say I'm too old; I do it. I'm happier at this time of my life. But look, I'm not ill. I don't have a broken hip, nor have I yet had a stroke. These things hover over older people, so I've been very fortunate that I can still work.

Whatever I do in life I've somehow made it interesting to me and amusing. If I'm washing dishes, which I don't often do, I try to enjoy it. I try to do it in such a way that it's fun to see the things come out sparkling. And, for instance, if I'm rushed and I don't want to fix a breakfast, I try to economize movement so it becomes almost a dance. I try to see that I make as few movements as possible and thereby become interested in the movement of getting breakfast rather than the deed, which is deadly boring.

I think that one can be creative wherever one is. You don't have to be an artist. The creative person is the person who is open to life and listening to life as it comes to him. You can be creative inside even as you're washing dishes. To me creativity is more a state of the inner being rather than the outer. There are lots of people who paint pictures who claim to be artists, but they're really not creative people. Many of them are very dull if you talk to them. They have no idea what the song of life is like. For the person shut up in a nursing home it must be very hard to think there's such a thing as the song of life. But, you know, there have been people who have gone through the most terrible imprisonments, isolation, torture, and they've come out wonderful human beings in spite of being just shut up in a box. Something inside of them has kept them alive, and I would say that it was their inward creativity.

There's no question that the outside of an individual

does change and wither and wrinkle, but very curiously the inside does not change and you will hear ever so many people say that. Even if they are old crocks, they will say, "I don't feel old." Age is very mysterious because the essence of the human being—the soul— actually never ages. It's only the outer covering of the individual that changes. For myself, I'm not at all concerned with age. I know I'm ninety because people tell me I'm ninety. Inwardly, I just laugh because, inwardly, I'm not in my nineties. I'm still sixteen or seventeen. And I have a very good time. I love getting in bed at night under the warmth of the electric blanket. I take a graham cracker with milk and I love it. I love looking at the mountains. And on a cold day I love getting into the hot tub. I think these are my greatest pleasures.

Life's a paradox. In one way, one knows what one wants and doesn't want, and in another way, one knows nothing of what one wants because the richness of experience opened up by the vastness of the universe tells us that we haven't a clue as to what we want. But life gives us choices. When one is young, one doesn't realize this. We think we can do this, do that, without wasting time. We don't realize that everything we choose builds up our life. Now that I'm an old binny I realize how important right choice really is. Now, some of us are born a little like ectoplasm; we haven't taken form yet. We have a purpose but we haven't found it yet, and so we lose time going into little eddies. Finally, we leave the eddy and come back to the big stream of living . . . with time we flow into the beautiful lake of peace.

As I said, this is the happiest time of my life. I would

say that if one has health it's really wonderful to grow old because one knows many things that one doesn't want. One can see the pattern of one's life where good things have happened and where silly things have happened. And let's hope that both things have happened to everybody, because it's good to have silly things happen. Let's say one is making soup, which is life. One begins with just a kettle of water. Now, if one only puts sugar in it, it's going to be sweet but it won't have a lot of character. If one adds a bit of salt and the silly things, it begins to have more taste. Then if one adds the vegetables of life—all the young men one has known that have broken one's heart—then it begins to really become a wonderful life. And the more one puts in incidents of life, lots of vegetables and such, the most wonderful soup develops.

I know the absurdity of old age because I've always hated old people, ever since I was young. When I was twenty-two a friend of mine who was twenty-five got married. And I thought to myself, "How could anyone marry such an old hag!" Then when I was fifty-eight a very nice woman of sixty-three was talking to me and I thought to myself, Oh, I don't want to talk to an old person like that. I've had to eat my words. Now I'm not the least bit concerned that I'm old.

My life is just full of mistakes, and they are like pebbles that make a good road. I remember, for example, that I was ill and had to go to the hospital for three days, mostly to rest. I found myself with an old, toothless hag who had an accent. I needed sleep, so I went to sleep. And this poor lady chatted and chatted. I was so mad. I tried to avoid her. The next day, after I had a little rest, I said to myself, I'm not nice to this poor woman. She needs somebody to talk to. I must be more decent to her. So when afternoon came I got off my high horse and listened to her. She'd had a heart attack, and she was all alone and frightened to death and in a state of crisis. The next day I was leaving. I whipped myself into a kind of decency and sat on her bed and talked to her. I said, "Look, I will speak to the doctor about you. When I leave I will phone every day." And that meant something to her. She felt absolutely bereft and alone. The day after leaving the hospital I left for Ventura and I was terribly tired, but I said to myself, I must go see that old woman. I sat on her bed and she appreciated it that I, a complete stranger, was befriending her. I sat on her bed, took her hand, and I looked at her, and to my astonishment this ugly old woman was beautiful. There was no wall between us. It was a wonderful experience.

You see, we're all really one, and that oneness between us I touched. When I left I said goodbye, and the next morning I phoned and they said I couldn't reach her. She died during the night. And it was wonderful for me, because I was sure she died knowing that somebody cared. Now you see the arrogance of the artist who did not want to be disturbed by the old hag. I threw that into the ashcan and met another human being. And that ugly human being became beautiful. This is one of the most important experiences and lessons of my life.

Richard Avedon

I first met Richard Avedon, one of America's leading photographers, in 1970 at the Minneapolis Institute of Arts, where his first exhibition of what he called his "deeper work" was being installed. Avedon had refused all media interviews, and the other reporters had given up and left. Avedon decided to take a break from supervising the mounting of his large black-and-white photographs and went outdoors to relax briefly under a tree. I tentatively approached him and asked nervously if I might join him. We chatted awkwardly for a few minutes, and then I asked the big question: "May I turn

283

on my tape recorder?" And that's how it happened: a level of comfort and confidence was established that has lasted over three decades.

Avedon's powerful, unembellished, black-and-white images have since been seen in many exhibitions and publications over the years. His portraiture, although favoring the conscious pose, is unadorned by mood lighting or props. The basic ingredients of his work have remained consistent over time: a white background, the sitter, the camera, and the photographer. His stark, powerful, and often controversial portraits include the anonymous and uncelebrated as well as the rich and famous. Avedon remains a very private person who prefers to spend his days in the studio working. However, as his reputation has grown, the photographer has become as much a focus of attention as his work.

M y first interview in the world was with you back in 1970. I had never done interviews before, and now you're talking to a media hack. I'm involved in something that is the enemy of artistic endeavor and creativity, which is self-promotion. It's important that I do it. It's in all my contracts now, for exhibitions and books, that I will promote myself, because if my books don't sell, there won't be another book or exhibit. So it's in my own best interests and in the interests of my work that I become this other person. But the me that talks about work and the me that does the work have very disparate qualities. When I'm doing work I can't talk about it. It's too fragile a process to play around with, and it's certainly too fragile to put into sound bites, to reduce my thoughts to fortune cookies, to be reductive about anything as complicated as making a work.

The one thing I believe in is that you work every day. If you're lucky enough to have a calling, if you're lucky enough to have something you want to do, you do it every day of your life. In the end, everything fades. Children grow up and go and have their own lives. Marriage, love, sex—everything diminishes, but work. When you're done, you have work. It's there, you did it. Anything you do well is who you are. That's the bottom line for me.

The way I live now is the way I've lived most of my adult life, after family life. I live above my studio, and I do some sort of work seven days a week. Before I moved in, my grandchildren's beds were in the room. They had a Civil War-era American flag on the wall, and there were photographs ranging from flying dolphins to sports pictures to Fred Astaire to photos of family and friends. The space (and my mind) was like a big junkyard. In some symbolic way I looked around and thought that the room was no longer my room. Magazine reporters and others came in here, and it became something that was no longer private, no longer my own world—as if the inside of my head had become public property.

So I took everything down and started over. And I created a room that has to do with this new and possibly last period of my life. I reinvented the room, and what is interesting is that where before it was chaotic, it now looks very neat, very precise. Every book, every clipping, all the things that didn't have meaning for me went out; all the junk, all the excess of everything that I once thrived on was pared down to a kind of calm. I needed a more organized life so I could access more passionate work.

I'm not taken in by my work. I'm not seduced by my work anymore. I'm not seduced by my success. I know that time is the competitor, that time really matters. It's a kind of stripping away of things that aren't essential. I'm not easily hurt anymore. I'm not as depressed as I was on and off when I was younger. I'm more demanding, maybe less considerate. I don't take other people's pain, or my own, as deeply as I took it ten years ago and before that. It's like, "Okay, it's tough, Dick. Pull up your socks and get on with it. And get on with it fast." I want to use this time as powerfully as I can. And if I look at the new work I do and I feel that it's fading, if it's an imitation of my past work, I'll tear it up and I will have taken my last photograph. The next ten years are a wrap for me. I don't necessarily mean in terms of my life but in terms of virility of mind and functioning in the way I've always functioned. What happens to me between eighty and ninety might be fun, but, as far as my work goes, every day matters because there aren't that many days left.

The thing that has become more difficult now is to tap my enthusiasms, my hungers, my drives, my ways of expressing my feelings, and put those into my work. My feelings themselves seem to be atrophying. I've began to cool, and my work is not cool work! I don't know exactly how those two things will find their way. I have very little interest in tranquility. Inner peace, spirituality, inner growth is just not who I am. Peace is nothing I aspire to. I'm just hoping to sustain the turmoil—to be questioning, to be anguished.

I'm a self-reflective, complex, and intense man. I've never liked the way I looked, but the older I get, the happier I am with the way I look. I've never liked my face. I didn't feel that it represented the guy inside. Now my face is beginning to look like the way I feel. I see the heaviness over my eyelids, and I like all the stuff that's happening to me. I'm beginning to look like an Avedon photograph! I hope that when I'm eighty, there'll be something there to photograph. It's like all the contradictions in me are no longer contradictory; they seem to be part of a whole that I recognize.

I didn't know that what wanes as I age is replaced by something that is infinitely wilder, stronger. I now can hold on to the emotional passion of what I once did on instinct alone, but I know what I'm doing. I know so much more now. It isn't just about craft; I'm wiser. I now find I work with more confidence, and my craft has become as subliminal as automatic writing. I know through experience so many things about photography. My technique of photography hasn't changed at all. There's been a common thread throughout. I've looked for the humanity in all the people I've photographed, the connections between a poet and a drifter, a pawnbroker and a model. If I hope for anything for my pictures it is that people will be able to look at them and see something serious that happened to life in our country in my time. As I get older it seems to me more important that I try to go back to one of the strongest parts of my youth: addressing the human condition. I don't mean that in some abstract, philosophical way. I mean it in terms of human needs. I came from a generation of people who believed that we could solve problems. I'll go on photographing what I think matters because that's the way I am.

I no longer know what art is about. I don't know who it reaches, I don't know what its purpose is, I don't know what it's for. What I do is all I know how to do, so I do it. If it were carpentry, I would do that, or running a business, I would do that. I don't know if art can change the world, but I do think and hope that someday some young person is going to go into a museum or open a book the way I did when I was young and find a piece of themselves that existed before their time. Find some kind of an affirmation that they're not alone. That's what art did for me when I needed it, and maybe that's what my work will do. My work now has a complete life of its own.

Mary Catherine Bateson

❧   ❧   ❧   ❧   ❧   ❧   ❧   ❧   ❧

Although her academic career has been in cultural anthropology, most recently at George Mason University and Harvard Graduate School of Education, it was at a conference dealing with the concept of "conscious aging" that I had an opportunity to speak with anthropologist, writer, and educator Mary Catherine Bateson. I had become acquainted with her writings in the early 1990s when a friend gave me a copy of her book, Composing a Life. *This book inspired one reader to write: "Mary Catherine Bateson was one of those pioneering women who helped me realize it is possible to change your* life." Bateson believes that our species survives by continually learning and that we learn from stories differently than we learn from generalities—a belief I share with her. What follows are some of Bateson's thoughts and reflections on aging, beginning with a memory of her mother, renowned cultural anthropologist Margaret Mead.

I have a memory that when my mother began to get gray hair, she was looking especially beautiful. It was a good time in her life, and she didn't disguise it. And I remember thinking how good my mommy looks. When I began to get gray hair, I looked in the mirror and thought, "I'm getting grow-it-yourself silver jewelry!" and I felt that I was going to look as pretty as I remember my mother looking. What a gift she had given me by not having disguised her own aging. I'm immensely fortunate to have had that. Many people have had parents who, as they aged, didn't have anything good to say or project about the aging process.

One of the problems that we women have, even more than men, is that we've been told all our lives that we don't conform to some ideal type. I remember reading *Seventeen* magazine when I was in my teens and knowing that I didn't look like that. It took quite a few years before I learned to look around and realize that my peers didn't look like that either, and, indeed, that the people I thought were beautiful didn't look like that. We're at risk of the same kind of process in thinking about aging. There's a stereotype that no woman is attractive over thirty. Terrible! This stereotype doesn't recognize the beauties of aging. And there's the risk of another stereotype—what I call the "super-elders"— people who are chronologically into their sixties and seventies and beyond but you wouldn't know it. They've just climbed Mt. Everest or accomplished some other physical feat. I look at the current magazines and think, "Here we go again. Somebody is telling me how I should look and how I should behave, and not only can I not do that, but it isn't me. It isn't my way of being productive or beautiful or vital."

I have a suspicion that the people who are best prepared for the aging process are those who sometime in their forties or fifties, before they feel like they're in a major midlife crisis, before they feel as if they're trapped, stop and take a breath, begin something new, take a long trip somewhere, a long thoughtful vacation, go back to school and learn a new skill, and say to themselves, "I have not committed myself to one adult role that I will hold on to until I despair of doing so." They say to themselves that they are growing, changing, learning, and being and that they live in a time of beginnings as well as endings. You adjust your expectations, you know what you're good at, and you don't waste your time trying to do what doesn't work for you.

If we're fortunate we can expect levels of health and energy that make the later years a different experience than they've been for previous generations. We're discovering, in a real sense, new stages of life that weren't available to people in the past. It is possible to open yourself to new information, feelings, ideas, learning. These are not material things. I often wonder what peo-

292 • Mary Catherine Bateson

ple mean when they say something is spiritual. What it is coming to mean to me is a changed quality of attention, both inward and outward. Listening, looking, tasting, meditating—it's all learning. I believe learning is a form of spirituality. Learning requires a degree of humility. You have to know that you don't know in order to learn something new. You have to know that you don't know as you walk through the woods in order to see something new around you. And you have to know that you need to be quiet and by yourself to let some new recognition grow within you. Now that's not a usual definition of spirituality and yet it seems to me that once you believe that all learning is a form of spirituality, it's a tremendously powerful connection to make. Simply to be willing to learn is to go into a sacred space. And take your shoes off before you go in!

Dr. Hunter "Patch" Adams

⧐ ⧐ ⧐ ⧐ ⧐ ⧐ ⧐ ⧐ ⧐

The real person behind the movie character "Patch Adams" is more than a medical doctor and a clown. Dr. Hunter is a serious social activist who criticizes the American health care system as expensive and elitist. Over thirty years ago, Dr. Hunter "Patch" Adams and a few of his like-minded colleagues founded the nonprofit Gesundheit Institute in northern Virginia. For a dozen years they operated a home-based family medical practice and managed to treat more than fifteen thousand people without payment, malpractice insurance, or formal facilities.

As the need for an actual physical facility grew, Adams shifted his focus to raising money to build his ideal hospital and to promote health and wellness on a global scale. From the start, it was imperative that fun and friendship be integrated into all medical care. The architect for the fee-free hospital was asked to make it a silly, playful place with trap doors, eyeball-shaped exam rooms, and chandeliers for swinging. Adams believes that life should be fun and that the healing interaction between patient and doctor should include joy, creativity, laughter, kindness, gentleness, and patience.

Adams's revolutionary kind of medicine takes time, the kind of time that rarely exists in today's productivity-driven doctor-patient relationships. "When a person comes to me," says Adams, "unless the problem is an arterial bleed that has to be addressed first, the goal is to have a friendship. We spend three to four hours in the first meeting. We might go for a walk, maybe we'll go fishing. By the end of our time together, I hope we have a trust and friendship."

When we met in his home office in Arlington, Virginia, Adams was wearing what he calls his "usual outfit": baggy clown pants, brightly colored suspenders, and a plaid shirt. When we began our conversation he told me, "It's invigorating to work for justice in health care, it's deeply thrilling. I've created a life where now, at age fifty-eight, I literally save lives everyday." The hospital is still on the drawing board, but Patch Adams is out in the world every day making people smile, telling his story, and planting seeds that may change forever the way health care is delivered.

The hospital doesn't exist as a building, an actual facility, but it does exist in practice. There are doctors who work with me who give up their malpractice insurance, doctors who now spend longer time with their patients. It's not likely I'll realize the dream of having the hospital in my lifetime. But keeping the dream alive feeds me every day and inspires people all over the world. What matters is holding on to the dream, living that dream. All the inspired people who work with the Gesundheit Institute and all the connections they've made in over forty countries keep the dream alive. The Robin Williams' movie about me sparked over three thousand groups and individuals to write to me. The movie inspired them to create projects in their own communities. I've gotten hundreds, thousands of letters from people saying, "We got your message, we're doing something!"

Loving is the most important thing in life. Yet I've gone all over the world and never found an elementary school, middle school, high school, or college that teaches loving. Our modern society is based on money and power, not compassion and generosity. There's no inspiration in the love of money, and no matter how much you have, it never seems to be enough. Only in surrendering to loving do you get "enough."

I teach loving by taking groups of people on a two-week clown tour of Russia. We clown. We put on clown clothes. You don't have to have any skills. We spend between ten to sixteen hours a day around the worst kind of poverty and suffering—and love, even deadened love, is awakened. We go to refugee camps. I've taken clowns into war three times, and I've clowned at maybe ten thousand deathbeds. I go to suffering. I give service because there's a call. Someone is hurt, you comfort them. You hear someone in pain and you say, "What can I do?" Service is vitality because love is vitality, and no matter how much you give, you never feel exhaustion.

Love is a thing that goes out from you, and you just keep giving it. It's an old-fashioned way of caring. It's not practical, it's not reimbursable, and it's not cost-effective. I know there are clowns in hospitals all over the world now. Clowning is a gimmick to get close to love. Clowning is fun. It was fun for me when I was a teenager, it was fun when I was in medical school, and it clearly is necessary and important in medical work. Along with miracle drugs I base my work on what Voltaire said, "The purpose of the doctor is to entertain the patient while the disease takes its course."

The future? I still want the hospital more than ever and the need for a hospital is greater than ever. The whole idea is using health care delivery as a tool to rebuild community. When we didn't get the hospital built, we could have quit, but I know we can keep doing good work, feel fulfilled, and inspire other people. The way to make things happen is through encouragement and inspiration. What else would I like to see happen in the world during the next decade? I'd want a world where no one alive could remember what the word "war" means. I hope to see the world protecting the natural environment. And I'd like to see money and power become insignificant things in life—maybe instruments for a way to care for all people.

The most revolutionary act you can commit in today's society is to be publicly happy. When I was eighteen, I decided to never have another bad day. I'm forty years into not having a bad day. It's a decision. I have no experience of boredom. I have no experience with a day that isn't fully inspired. Life inspires. I taste life much better at age fifty-eight than I did at fifty-seven. I've just had the best year of my life, and I think this every year because I'm continually growing and expanding in every direction. Wisdom comes with experience, time, and age. Wisdom was once thought to be the gift of age. Wisdom is not something that's considered important in our society now. Now we want to inject Botox and get rid of wrinkles, deny that age exists. Wrinkles meant you had lived, that you were there. What I can say about age is that if you're alive, if you're vital, then growing older is additive. You can remember, you can anticipate, you can continue to learn and grow.

For me, life inspires. I haven't had a long and hard journey. I haven't had a difficult journey. Life is experience, and I love every second. For me life is swimming in an ocean of gratitude, love, joy, humor, wonder, curiosity, passion, hope and creativity, and never finding the shore.

Susan Stamberg

❯ ❯ ❯ ❯ ❯ ❯ ❯ ❯ ❯

Broadcast journalist Susan Stamberg is well known for her conversational approach, her knack for finding an interesting story, and her fresh, friendly, down-to-earth style. For over thirty years her voice has been familiar to millions who listen to National Public Radio. In the early 1970s she became the first woman to anchor a nightly news program, and for fourteen years she served as co-host of the award-winning All Things Considered. She's won every major award in broadcasting, has been inducted into the Broadcasting Hall of Fame and the Radio Hall of Fame, and has received many other awards and numerous honorary degrees. I've known Susan Stamberg for over thirty years. When I asked if she would talk with me about the challenges and changes she'd faced in recent years, she replied, "You've been talking about this aging thing for years now, but I've finally caught up!"

I'm 65 now. I went to the social security office, fully expecting them to say, "Don't be silly, miss. You're not qualified yet. Go away." But they just said, "Here are the papers, fill them out." I'm not the same "old" as my mother was at sixty-five. When my parents were sixty-five, they were really old. They were old even in their forties. Now getting old is quite different. On the other hand, I've got this arthritic hip that keeps talking to me, and when it hurts I do feel my age. The hip and the different way my memory works, or doesn't work, make me aware that things have changed for me. I'm really much slower than I used to be. My mind is slower. I sometimes reach for words. The suppleness I had in thinking and writing sentences that please me, I'm losing some of that.

A few times over the years I dyed my hair, but I've made a commitment to silver and now I'm leaving my hair as it is. My hair has a lot of curl to it, and when I dyed it, it went lank and terrible. I think it's quite beautiful now the way the light hits it, and the upkeep is much cheaper if I just let it be the way it is. I think I look good, even better now than when I was younger. A commitment to exercise and keeping as fit as you can is very important. Eating right. And most of all, attitude. People should stay active and involved. That doesn't mean staying young, but staying engaged and interested. It's important to be realistic and be the truth of what we are. That's why I'm against all that cosmetic stuff—the whole beauty thing in our country and the youth culture stuff. I'm politically, emotionally, and psychologically opposed to doing Botox and trying to stop the passage of time. I think I've earned every wrinkle I have. As Ingrid Bergman said once, "At forty you get the face that you deserve, and by sixty-five you're even more of who you are."

I'm no longer on a daily program at National Public Radio, so I don't have a regular staff that I work with intimately day after day. But being busy and occupying my mind, having a place to go every day, really means a lot to me. Even when I took time out from producing pieces for radio to write a book, NPR gave me an office, so that even if I closed the door to write, I was in a place that had a real buzz of activity. That's very important to me. After I left a daily program it took me years to wind down and not feel guilty about not being productive as I had been. Every once in a while I'll say to myself, "I'm only doing one story a week. That's not really right. It's not enough. Blah, blah, blah." But I don't think about what contribution other people are making to the world anymore. That certainly was a measure of mine when I was younger. I don't come at people in that way anymore. That's a difference that age has made, and a difference that I like. It doesn't seem quite as judgmental. I look at others more as a whole person and the pleasure and satisfaction they get out of small things rather than on the world stage. I used to think about not being "productive" with a certain horror, but now I don't see things that way at all. I can now understand the pleasures of slowing down.

This past year my mother died at the age of ninety-seven. She had moved here to Washington from New York after my father died. I'm an only child, and I was responsible for her. She lived in her own apartment until the age of ninety-five. During those years I traveled around and gave a lot of speeches to earn extra money to pay for companions and other help for her. Eventually we moved her into a nursing home very close to us. She rallied from one disease after another. I guess that's why I figured she wasn't going to die. But, at her age, I realized that I was going to lose her, and I thought I was prepared for her death. Yet, I am utterly amazed at how deeply I'm feeling her loss. She was a wonderful, wonderful mother, and we always had a good relationship. She was sweet and loving as a mother. It's her presence that I miss, and knowing that my whole life she was there for me. I'm now the elder in the family. It's painful, I miss her, and it makes me extremely sad. Yet, it's enriching in many ways when I think about her. It's nourishing to me, pleasing to me. In this way she's still with me.

I know I'm not going to get old in the same way my mother did. For the last ten years of her life she never left her apartment. She wouldn't go out with us. It seemed a very lonely and isolated life. I've resolved that I'm never going to do this to myself. When the time comes that I'm not the me I want to be anymore, I'm really going to take a pill. I'm very serious about this. I have no intentions of living a diminished life. When I think about my mother I look back and realize that for maybe the last thirty years of her life she became more and more anxious. Now I'm beginning to see some of that anxiety and worry in myself. Like today I didn't want to go out because there's ice on the streets and I was afraid I might slip. But I'm a fighter and I plunge ahead, and when my time comes I hope that's still there in me.

I've been married forty-two years. Our relationship has evolved and grown as we've gone through different stages of our life. At one time we both had very busy careers and we raised a child. My husband, Lou, retired from the Department of State's Agency for International Development after a thirty-four-year career. Since then our marriage has had an interesting shift, and to my mind, so much for the better. I had worried a lot about him in his retirement. Lou wasn't a man with a lot of hobbies or outside interests. But he's extraordinary. He's the most successful retired person I know. He has this wonderful energy about him, and he's much more relaxed than when he worked. He's blossomed in a million ways. He has time for people now, and he takes time to go to lunch and talk with people. Lou is part of a program that reads the daily newspapers to the blind. He's on a number of boards and think tanks. I've noticed that he has less and less time to do the things he did when he first retired, which was do the marketing and cook. He loves his retirement, but sometimes I say to him, "You can't take on another thing. You really don't have the time. And what about dinner?"

Lou takes French lessons, and he's gotten very good at the language. Now we go to France twice a year. They say the best way to keep a brain from aging is to learn a new language. I used to be the one that did the talking because I can fake an accent, but now he has the grammar and the vocabulary, so he's become the communicator when we're there. He's become involved in a million things. I can't see that for myself. I can only see me continuing to work and to do what I do. His retirement has been a huge change. When we were younger, whatever energies we had went into our careers. After that came child-raising and child care. And after that was tending to our marriage. Now it's a big shift. I'm far more dependent on Lou than I ever was, and he, I would say, is in a better blend of dependency.

At National Public Radio, I get a certain kind of respect. I'm not as easily dismissed as an older person might be in another kind of work situation. I don't think I'm really up to the kind of trudging and traveling that I used to do to get a story for broadcast. My hip keeps talking to me, and I know I'm going to have to do something about it. I notice lately that sometimes when I get together with my long-time friends the first topic of our conversation is our health. I used to notice this with older people and hated it, and now here I am.

Lou is much better than I am these days at keeping the engine oiled. He'll say, "Let's go do this." I look at him with envy sometimes and wonder, if I didn't have NPR to go to every day, would I be self-motivated? All my life I have been, but I'm not sure I have that anymore. I ask myself, "Would it be enough just to *be* rather than always having things to *do?*" How would I feel about that? Would it make me depressed, keep me housebound? Or would I find other pleasures and satisfactions? I don't know the answer. I'm not there. But I'm a little concerned about it.

Lou said that by the time he was seventy he wanted to be out of the house. He didn't want the responsibility of fixing gutters and hot water heaters and things like that. So we looked around at apartments and realized that anything we liked would cost us more than we could get for this house, and to go into debt at this point in our lives seemed nuts. So we stopped looking, and that's why we got the painters in and did a fix-up in the house and re-did the floors and freshened it all up. We didn't go so far as to put in an elevator. I can't imagine moving out of our house now. And I sure can't imagine moving to another city and making a new life. Moving takes a lot of energy that I don't have anymore, so I'll stay where I am.

One of the best things for me about getting older is that I've eased up on myself. I think when I was younger I worked so hard. I was very driven to succeed. Nothing was good enough. I just pushed and pushed and pushed. Now I've come to a time in my life when I don't feel I have to do that anymore. I can ease up and look around and see the things I've accomplished. It's not sitting on my laurels, but it's using them to step into a more comfortable place. Maybe that's the way to put it. I hope that's maturity, not just being tired. I have a pretty good attitude. I think of myself as very mature, very grown-up. No matter what the day brings, I try to have one good experience a day. Sometimes that means just having a coconut cookie!

Andrew Weil

❧   ❧   ❧   ❧   ❧   ❧   ❧   ❧   ❧

In a cover story in the May 12, 1997 edition of Time magazine, Dr. Andrew Weil summed up his attitude towards medicine and healing: "There's a lot that conventional medicine does well, and in many cases, it's just what's called for. If I'm in a car accident, don't take me to an herbalist. If I have bacterial pneumonia, give me antibiotics. But when it comes to maximizing the body's natural healing potential, a mix of conventional and alternative procedures seems like the only answer."

Dr. Weil, a Harvard-educated physician, is recognized worldwide as a leading exponent of alternative medicine. He *claims he never wanted to be an alternative medicine guru, yet for several years he's been a trailblazer in the field now known as "integrative medicine." I've had an interest in Dr. Weil's work for some time, yet my motivation for talking with him was to find out more about him personally. Because he thinks innovatively about medicine, I thought he might have some innovative thoughts about aging as well.*

I'm 61 now. My health is pretty good. I've never had any major illnesses. I'm very careful about diet. I make sure I get regular exercise. I take vitamins. I practice sitting meditation. And most days I do breathing exercises. I have the usual twinges and aches, but I don't have any major problems. There was a period in my thirties when I ran, but then I got pretty clear signals from my body that it didn't want to do that, so I now swim a lot, which agrees with me.

I thought turning fifty was going to be the big watershed in my life, but it wasn't. Sixty was. There was something about turning sixty that made me aware that I was entering a different phase of life. My contemporaries and I all have a sense of "How did we get here? How astonishing that we're in our sixties!" My friends and I are thinking seriously about how we want to spend the remaining years that we have. We're obsessed with how we want to be in our later years, particularly around the issues of community and connectedness. We don't want to live in retirement communities, but we do want to live around our friends. Some of my friends are talking about creating a community where we all have our own spaces but have communal cooking and dining. I think that's an interesting plan.

I have a lot of freedom in how I design my life. It's important for me to live in areas that have wilderness, where I can enjoy natural beauty, relatively clean air, and where I can garden. I still make my living mostly as a writer. I'm actively involved in teaching, but I don't want to do that forever. However, it's difficult for me not to be obsessed with work. My work seems to bleed into all aspects of my life, what with e-mails, faxes, and cell phones. I have to make a really conscious effort to disengage for periods of time. It gets harder and harder. I tend to be a perfectionist. It's very difficult for me to let go of things, but I have too much to do now. One way I'm able to get some balance is by delegating, which is a difficult thing for me to do. I've had to learn that I can't be in control of everything. I now work with others on my newsletter, website, and university program.

I find it very important to do things for myself that raise my spirits. This means spending time with people in whose company I feel alive and connected. I spend time in nature. These things are important and beneficial to my spiritual health. I hesitate to recommend a specific activity for others. It's different for different people. I can give some general suggestions, like trying to keep fresh flowers in your presence, listening to music that elevates your spirit, and spending more time with people in whose company you feel better. I find as I get older that friends are more and more important to me, and I'm really selective about them.

I don't want to waste time with people in whose company I feel agitated or depressed. I have less and less patience for this.

It's a striking characteristic of our culture that we live in denial of aging. We invest a tremendous amount of time, money, and energy in cosmetic surgery and anti-aging preparations. There's a tremendous desire not to face the reality of aging. Our culture values youth and devalues aging. But people don't have to age in the way their parents did.

What makes for healthy aging, productive aging? A MacArthur Foundation study that was done a few years ago found two outstanding characteristics in a large group of healthy older people. The first was maintenance of physical activity throughout life. This did not necessarily mean going to aerobics classes; it just meant being physically active in some way every day. The second was active intellectual and social connectedness. This certainly fits with my experience. I think that these are far and away the most important determinants of how people age. These characteristics overshadow nutrition, use of vitamins, and other factors.

It's easy to keep physically active; it's harder to stay connected. In our culture there's a tendency for older people to become isolated and to spend most of their time with other older people. This is something we really have to guard against. We need to figure out ways to interact with people of different ages and maintain connections with the world. In our culture you really have to work to make community happen. You really have to guard against isolation.

Something I find very discouraging when I'm in the homes of older people is to see how many prescription drugs are there, often a dozen or more. Older people in our culture are becoming more and more dependent on prescription medicines, and I don't think that's a good thing. As a practitioner of integrative medicine and natural medicine, I think it's often desirable to use fewer of these things, not more of them. In many cases people are not aware of the interactions between these medications. I don't mean they should be denied access to medical care, but I'd like to see older people become more independent of medications and more self-reliant.

I'm trying to train doctors when to use conventional medicine and when not to, how to combine these other systems and when not to. Doctors and pharmacists can be trained, though at the moment we're really not training people to guide patients through this confusing maze. Some medical schools are moving in this direction. What individual patients can do is let their physicians know what they want and also help them broaden their education. I've had many patients who have told me they've introduced other doctors to herbal medicine, new ideas in nutrition, or some of the other things that aren't currently taught in medical schools. I think this is an idea whose time has come.

Ever since I began training doctors in this new field of integrative medicine, there has been an enormous emphasis on listening to people. A very high percentage of the patients that come through our clinic at the University of Arizona say that this the first time they've had a chance to tell their story to a doctor. They say it's the first time a doctor has really listened to them. From my own clinical practice, I've found the most powerful diagnostic instrument to be the patient's medical history. But you have to have time to ask questions, you have to know how to ask questions, and you have to listen. If you do these things, you can get at the root causes of most people's problems and where you can intervene.

Aging is an interesting journey. It's good to be conscious of it. Conscious aging means not denying it. Denial is probably the greatest trap that I see people fall into. Denial of aging is insidious, pervasive. It's catered to by many forces in our society. It's really important to wake up and take charge. Probably, when I hit my seventies, I'll have another awakening.

When I look at something and see how it is, I always think that maybe I can find a different way. That's the way my mind works. Part of me is always questioning. I certainly have always carved my own path and marched to my own drummer. I feel very lucky to have been able to do this.

Walter Mondale

❧   ❧   ❧   ❧   ❧   ❧   ❧   ❧   ❧

Walter Mondale has an office in the law firm of Dorsey & Whitney in downtown Minneapolis. I was scheduled to meet with him in a comfortable, wood-paneled conference room. I set up my tape recorder and waited for him to arrive. I first met Walter Mondale in his senate office in Washington, D.C., in the 1960s when my husband and I took our three young children to the nation's capital to see the sights and meet their senator. Years later, when Walter Mondale was vice president, I was the cultural reporter at National Public Radio and had another opportunity to meet both him and his wife, Joan, who was a national advocate for the arts.

Walter "Fritz" Mondale has been involved in politics since the end of World War II. He helped Hubert H. Humphrey get elected to the U.S. Senate in 1948, and, when Humphrey was chosen to be Lyndon Johnson's vice president, Mondale replaced Humphrey in the Senate. Mondale was reelected in 1966 and 1972, served as vice president under Jimmy Carter in 1976, and ran for president against Ronald Reagan in 1980. In 1993 President Clinton appointed him U.S. Ambassador to Japan.

It wasn't easy to get on Walter Mondale's calendar. He's active in Democratic politics, speaks on many issues, serves on both non-profit and corporate boards, and teaches, lectures, and writes.

I 'm now what they call "senior counsel" here at the law firm. I advise, but I'm not in the intensive twelve-hour-a-day competitive world that I lived in for most of my life. This is a new balance of work and leisure. I can do things at the edges, still be involved talking to people, and it's actually quite comfortable. I don't have to go to all the meetings. I have a wonderful secretary, and my wife, Joan, helps me. I have more than one thing going on at a time, so I do need some help to get it done and be efficient and not forget what I've promised to do—and not miss my grandson Louie's ball game today at four o'clock!

I'm 76 now; the odometer just turned. When you're young, you're healthy and strong. You're as alert as you're ever going to be. You're jumpy about getting from here to there in a hurry. You can get along on four hours sleep. Your schedule is endless. You're impatient and you're in a rush. I now balance my time far differently than when I was younger. I don't have a great strategic plan, but I try to figure out a day ahead of me what I think I can do.

As you reach your retirement years, your older years, if you're lucky you've got good health, you're still reasonably alert, you've got a family, you've got relationships, and all that can make it very nice. But you also are out of the competitive world, the intense working world. Priorities change. I'm not in the fast race anymore.

Not having to work twelve to fourteen hours a day, that seems to me like a gift. I like being around my children and my grandchildren, yet able to walk away when the heavy work starts. That wasn't true when we were raising our families. I feel very fortunate because I can shape my life the way I want to, be close to those who are working, to read and participate in things—like tomorrow when I'm going to speak to a group on preserving the wild and scenic river system in America. I was involved in these issues when I was a senator and also when I was vice president.

I was in politics forever it seems—from 1946 until 2003. When I stepped off the political stage, it was something I more or less expected, and I find I'm living with it all right. I was in public life longer than most person's working careers. It's not as though I was cheated. It isn't frustrating for me not to be as involved as I have been in the past. I've had a full quota. When you think about aging rationally, you know that it's coming, that these changes in life are to be expected.

There are cycles in life. Now I spend a lot of time working on issues, on my lecture series, and on public and civic affairs. That's what I try to do. I feel a very strong sense of responsibility towards others.

This morning I was at a meeting about the coming presidential election. We talked about the campaign. Doing these kinds of things keeps me involved. But I'm not the candidate, so it's different. I was in the Senate race after Paul Wellstone's death. I thought it was worth the challenge and the risk, but I never would have run at age seventy-five for a six-year term except that the tragedy and the circumstances of Paul Wellstone's death required it. You're making some bets at my age that things will work out well. I think they would have. I've tried to keep active in things that interest me. It's not like I have idle hands.

I spend a lot of time talking to my friends who are in public life or have been in public life. I spend a lot time reading. I do a lecture series at the university here called the Minnesota Community Project. I'm involved in the presidential campaign. I talk with the current candidates and the people around them. I speak out on these things. In other words I haven't quit expressing myself when I really want to say something. I'm not out there every day like I once was, but I try very hard to be current, to understand, to encourage things I believe in and discourage things I'm negatively concerned about.

Leisure for me is reading, going to see our grandchildren, family vacations, fishing, hunting, politics, meeting with old friends. Reminiscing is important for me. I like to be with old friends. We find ourselves talking about the good old days, the bad old days, that sort of stuff. You start thinking more about the next generation as you look at your grandchildren, your other friends in the community. Where is it going to go? What did we do? What should we have done? I'm very worried about the war we're in. I'm worried about the weakening ability of communities to educate the next generation, which is crucial to our future. These sorts of things worry me a lot. Oh sure, I have regrets. I very much regret that I wasn't able to get Jimmy Carter get reelected as president. I live with that. I guess I also regret that I couldn't win the election to fulfill serving Paul Wellstone's term in the Senate.

People sometimes come up to me and thank me for what I've done or what I've said or let me know that their daughter is running for public office because of me. Yes, I get a lot of that, and it's really wonderful. That's one of the dividends you get for having been in public life and having tried to help others. It's nice that while you're still living people express their appreciation.

You sure learn a lot when you live a long time, whether you want to learn things or not! It's not only what you read, but what you live through, the tremendous range of experiences in your personal life, your family life, and your friends' lives. It's almost impossible to summarize what this means, but as you get older you get this feeling that all of that accumulative knowledge may be worth something—and I think it is. There is a thing called wisdom. But I think you have to temper wisdom with generational change. Each new generation is going to do it their way. They'll listen to grandpa, but we're advisors, not commanders, not parents. They're going to shape their lives in this world their way, just as we did in our time. So I think part of wisdom is to give everybody plenty of room and not try to crowd the scene. You got to let go a little bit as you're participating. Otherwise your grandchildren and younger people are going to stay away from you.

A sense of humor is a blessing and the biggest necessity in life. With it life is more fun, more bearable, and you're more bearable than you would be otherwise. How you end up making judgments, conclusions, drawing advice for others—a good sense of humor helps balance your perspective.

When you're younger and you're working full-time and you're working hard and doing well on your job, you have status. When you meet someone for the first time, you ask, "What do you do?" That's how we position each other. As you get older and you start moving away from that job and that structure and that pacing, you have to adjust. You need to deal with that and accept it. It's not an insult. God's not playing a trick on you. It's just the way things work. Don't take yourself too seriously. Take what you're doing seriously, but don't be hard on yourself. I'm a talented malingerer! I move along the way it feels that day, and I think people accept it. What people see in me, where I am in life, is greatly different from what they saw fifteen years ago, I know that. You should be able to feel good about yourself. You should be able to manage the changes in you as you age.

I've got a good family, and I'm busy the way I want to be. We love our grandchildren. Last night I went to a hockey game. This afternoon I'm going to a basketball game. We do a lot of that. It's wonderful to see the kids play, to be around them in circumstances where they're having a good time, to watch them grow physically and intellectually, to have that family life. It's wonderful. What you can do for your grandchildren and for their children and what they can do for you is one of the valuable things in life. I don't know how families handle it when they live thousands of miles apart. Fortunately, our grandchildren live here in the same town. I'm very glad to be a grandparent. It's one of the joys of my life. And then there's the question of how a grandparent should behave. I think, carefully. Be helpful, give advice, be around when you're needed, try to be friend, but be careful not to scold or be a "big foot." I don't think that works. I don't think parents can deal with that. Grandchildren can't deal with that.

My theory is that you have to accept the aging process. Don't take yourself too seriously. Try to keep your mind going, I think that's important. If you withdraw, stay home all the time, don't get around, you start losing it. You have to accept what happens to you, what will happen to you. One's health certainly takes up more time when you're older—thinking about it, taking care of it, visiting the doctor, that sort of thing. Your body ages, your stamina levels begin to fade. I bet everyone my age has a similar story to tell, maybe different details. I know I'm getting older, one year at a time, and Joan and I have tried to make adjustments so that these later years are comfortable, dignified, and we're doing what we want to do. We don't turn off all the switches. We try to keep a pace and an interest level and an involvement that we find comfortable. I wouldn't want to relive my earlier years again. Aging happens, and you need to accept this natural evolution in your life, as everyone else has had to. You'll be happier if you do.

Peter Yarrow

≫   ≫   ≫   ≫   ≫   ≫   ≫   ≫   ≫

Peter Yarrow and his singing partners in the trio Peter, Paul and Mary have over the years committed their time and talent in support of such causes as equal rights, peace, the environment, gender equality, homelessness, hospice care, and education. They have often used their music to convey messages of humanity and caring. Now Peter Yarrow has a new project.

At age sixty, Yarrow began Operation Respect, an ambitious program for children and youth aimed at reducing and eliminating bullying behaviors. Yarrow talks passionately of creating ridicule-free zones in his school-based programs. He *describes Operation Respect as a tool for building community, catalyzing change, and inspiring youth.*

I'm 65 now, and this is probably is the most important work of my life. Most of my years as an adult have been focused on trying to make sure that the efforts of society advance the human condition in one way or another. Certainly, that was my reason for becoming involved in the antiwar and environmental movements. These were attempts to try to right societal wrongs by changing institutions and laws to reflect the values of compassion, humanity, and fairness.

But this is a very difficult way to make change that sustains. Real work has to be done in the hearts of young children and young adults first. You can change institutions, but people's consciousness—their internal value systems and prejudices and biases—don't necessarily change. We're living in times antithetical to what democracy is all about. How do we counter this?

If kids can grow up to respect themselves and others for who they are intrinsically, they can go on to become peacemakers, citizens that make the world a fairer and more just place. The name of the game is empowerment and self-respect. Cycles of hatred, bias, and powerlessness must be interrupted in the young. That's what Operation Respect intends to accomplish. It is an attempt to change the educational paradigm in America so that the social and emotional growth of kids is considered with the same seriousness as academics. The growth of a young person's ethical spirit should be considered as much a part of the teacher's charge as teaching math and science.

Do you know that somewhere around 160,000 children stay home from school daily because of fears of bullying? One part of Operation Respect is something called the "Don't Laugh at Me" program. When I introduce the program to teachers, counselors, and others involved in youth-based programs, I sing "Don't Laugh at Me" by Steve Seskin and Allen Shamblin. The song is very powerful. "Don't laugh at me," goes the chorus, "Don't call me names / Don't get your pleasure from my pain / In God's eyes we're all the same."

Initially I thought that when I sang "Don't Laugh at Me" I was just sensitizing listeners to the disrespect that exists in children's lives. I thought I was motivating and mobilizing them to do their part to change things. What I ultimately realized was that something deeper was happening. Teachers and counselors told me that my song reminded them why they went into their choice of work in the first place. They responded with enthusiasm to integrating the "Don't Laugh at Me" program into their curriculum. Many told me that they once again felt hopeful, idealistic, and determined that they could actually have an effect. It rekindled the belief that if we stand together, we can move a mountain.

In another song you've probably heard are the words, "you've got to be taught to hate and fear." People learn to be biased, intolerant, and racist. Before such learning happens we need to give kids the tools to interact compassionately, to recognize the value of their own feelings, to interact with a sense of mutual acceptance, and to respect themselves and others. The goal is to know that they are not defined by the brand of their sneakers or their parent's wealth or the size of the house they live in.

Can older persons change the perspective of how they view themselves? As we age we also need to reinforce our feelings of self-worth and respect for self and others. The name of the game for older people is empowerment and self-respect as well. I know things now that I never could have known before. I really have a sense of the forest rather than just the trees—the big picture.

I think that it's up to people individually to know that it's their task to define themselves in such a way that they don't have to prove their vitality; they just have to be vital. If they don't feel it then they've bought into this societal perception of people who are aging as being disposable. The point is that we have to confound the stereotype of aging by living differently. The greatest advocacy we can bring to change is our example—realize what our lives can be, and not worry about how we're perceived but concentrate on how we view ourselves. I think that if people are not directly and usefully engaged in what they love, their capacity to grow is diminished.

I'm older chronologically, sure. You see these paintings on my wall here? Some are from the 18th and 19th centuries. They're old. They're old—and wonderfully so. "Old" need not be a pejorative word. I don't feel old in the sense of being worn out, no longer at my peak. I have a different kind of peak now. And that's where my energies should go. I don't try to compete on the ski slopes with thirteen-year-olds. I'm trying to mature in an on-going sense. The reality is that you can say, "I have the great joy of doing whatever I want to do now."

I work in hospice. I go there and sing. And when I sing for people in hospice care it's the most spiritual kind of sharing that I've ever done. Every single time that's the case. When you're with people who have a very limited time, for whom every moment counts in a special way, there is no place for artifice. There's only room for love and truthful exchange. These people are reaching for what is truly important in life, and it's amazing. It's some of the most powerful living I've ever observed.

I feel everyday that I'm in the most exciting period of my life. That probably sounds absurd to younger people. I have the most vibrant relationships and I'm doing the most meaningful work of my life. I see myself as a work in progress, and I'm continually excited by new possibilities as I continue to grow and gain wisdom and a greater appreciation for what life is truly about. I'm not just doing the same thing I always did without changing and evolving. I continue to learn and see things from different perspectives.

Mike Martin

Kitty Carlisle Hart

❧ ❧ ❧ ❧ ❧ ❧ ❧ ❧ ❧

Kitty Carlisle Hart's career has spanned more than seventy years. She was fifty-four when she made her debut at the metropolitan Opera and sixty-four when she became the chairperson of the Arts Council of New York. Television watchers remember her fondly from the years she was a regular on the panel show To Tell the Truth. Her marriage to playwright/director Moss Hart were years of gaiety, ball gowns, dinner parties, and the glamorous world of Broadway theater. Moss Hart died in 1961.

Kitty Carlisle Hart says that her greatest success is that she's still working at ninety-one. "I'm both mentally and physically active," she told me when we spoke. "I get on the floor and do my exercises four times a week. I can put my feet over my head and touch my feet behind me, come down and do thirty leg lifts. I've been doing that all my life."

I asked her what her advice was for keeping busy.

I never say "no" to anything. Saying "yes" has made a wonderful life for me. Every once in a while I look up at the ceiling and say, "I need help. I don't have enough work. Help me!" And somehow it works, the phone rings. I'm always looking for more work. I never say "no" to anything that's offered.

About six years ago I got a call from the man who runs the Metropolitan Museum. He told me he was planning a series called "Art New York," and he wanted me to help create the part on the American musical theater. And then he said these fatal words: "And we'll get someone to sing your songs for you." The truth was, I hadn't sung in twenty years, so I said to myself, "I have to get back in shape." I decided to take on performing and singing in eight weeks of summer stock theater. I worked hard and I got my voice back, and then I knew I could sing my part in the Met's musical theater program. That was the beginning. And now, suddenly, I'm booked all over the country.

How old am I? I'm 93. I'm touring with the show that I developed, My Life on the Wicked Stage. I just got back from Tampa and I'm going off again soon to Kansas City and then to Columbus. And I'm doing a week here in New York too.

You know, you can do more than you think you can. You have to find something that really interests you and you have to pursue it ferociously. It doesn't have to be work that pays, but it has to be something that you do every single day. I remember a time when I took on every kind of volunteer job that I could find. I was on the board of the Red Cross, and the Third Street Music School, and this one and that one, and eventually I found out what I really wanted to do and took on the job heading the New York State Arts Council. I think everyone should just give things a try. I tell people that they must never stop. Never say that you're too old for this or that. You'll see—we can all do more than we think we can.

John Lahr

❧　❧　❧　❧　❧　❧　❧　❧　❧

In 1969 John Lahr wrote what is widely considered one of the best show business biographies ever written: Notes on a Cowardly Lion, the story of the life and career of Lahr's vaudeville comedian father, Bert Lahr. Since 1992, Lahr has been a theater critic and profile writer for The New Yorker magazine. He has also written or edited twenty-five books of essays, biographies, play anthologies, stage adaptations, screenplays, and novels.

I first met John Lahr in the 1960s when he was the dramaturge at the Guthrie Theater in Minneapolis. We tried to

332 • John Lahr

keep in touch over the years, but somewhere along the way, as often happens, contact was lost. One day as I was reading The New Yorker I realized that a conversation with John Lahr would make a thoughtful addition to this book. I tracked him down easily with a phone call. It was a happy reunion, and within a couple of weeks we were sitting in his office as he shared his thoughts and experiences.

I want to tell you a story. When I was about ten or eleven, my father and I were fishing in Canada. It was a hot day. My father was trolling, and I was really bored. I was sitting with the Indian guide in the back, fooling around, and I put my hand in the lunch basket and pulled out a boiled egg. I dropped the egg in the water and watched it slowly, elliptically, start to drop and go deep and deeper and deeper until suddenly it disappeared. I broke out in a sweat. I realized that someday I was going to disappear, die. That was the informing moment of my entire life because I realized that I didn't want to waste a second of it. In my mind that egg was a bit like a Latin dance of death. The negative always informs the positive and focuses the moment. I see the whole ethos of denial and escape in American thinking. In a culture in which life is everything, death doesn't fit in. What happens in America, and I feel it so strongly, is that if the whole enterprise of life is invested in what I'd call "the destiny of me," and if the "me" doesn't exist, it's intolerable. Europeans just don't understand this about Americans. They look upon American optimism as a kind of mutation, a kind of madness. In England where I live now, they tell a joke about death. They say that a European's death is inevitable and an American's is optional.

There is so much to do and so little time. I'm sixty-two now. I've written eighteen books, some plays, and some movies. I've had lots of downs with the ups. I had a tragedy in the 1980s. My former wife and I had twins that died at birth. They were born prematurely. One died in two days and the other lived for two weeks. Had the child lived, he would have been blind, unable to walk, and brain-damaged. I remember thinking that this kind of loss has to mean something. I watched him during those two weeks, and it made me realize how smug human beings are about existence. Because of this experience I connected with the miraculous in the everyday. The nature of maturity is holding the pluses and the minuses together. Suffering and loss are part of life. I've learned to live with loss and to absorb it, and that has helped me define who I am.

I've had a very lucky life. Maybe the luckiest thing was having this tragedy because it made me seize my day. I try to make every day as valuable to me as I can. My life with my wife of the last fifteen years has been just magical. We moved into a house this summer. I've never owned a house before. It's sort of a miracle to me that a freelance writer could have a house and a garden in England where the prices are really high. I've been working here at The New Yorker for eleven years, and I think in those years there have been maybe one or two days when I haven't put out 110 percent and gotten back 110 percent. I write for approximately 900,000 people a week. *The New Yorker* magazine is a perfect place for what I do. I write about theater at length, interview and profile people, and discuss their work. I really want to keep the dialogue of theater artists going in the culture. For a writer it's a bit like landing in Oz. So many people here are working to polish you up, you look pretty good at the end of a day. You've got a lot of help. Everyone here wants the same thing: literary excellence. It gives you a lot of confidence to know that, if you make a mistake, someone here will find it and without acrimony happily help you. Putting words together and making them have proper impact and spin is such a fascination for me. Everyday is a learning experience. It's exciting and thrilling, and I work hard at it.

If we're lucky, there's a time in our lives when we wake up and realize that we're not going to live forever. Maybe it's something about age and harmony, becoming awake to the world and ourselves. I'm always startled at how spellbound and enchanted American culture is. You know things are going along okay, you're comfortable, but you're not really alive. I'm not talking about any particular kind of formal religion but the appreciation of the miraculous, which is right in front of our eyes, yet transparent. Like right now. You're looking into my eyes, and I'm looking into yours. You don't even think about it, unless you don't have sight. You'd better deal with your issues, you better love the people that you love, you better do the work that you want to do, and you better honor the miracle of it all.

I've been thinking about the story of the egg that I told you, about the mystery of the miraculous. I was trout fishing a couple of years ago. I was standing in deep water, and there was a gorgeous yellow and black butterfly. I followed it as it darted and eddied. It came down right in front of me and then it disappeared. It was so beautiful, and I thought, "Well, that's it. The river is time, and time sweeps up all gorgeous things." I think in the theater you get this insight from great playwrights. They're aware, and they're trying to help you defeat some of the inevitable despair of leaving the earth, to accept it and see yourself as not the center of everything but as part of the cycle, the whole.

My long-term project is a biography of Tennessee Williams. I was asked to do this ten years ago, but only now am I really up to doing Williams, I think. What would I have known back then about the kind of suffering Williams was writing about? Now I've lived in the world enough to ask different questions of the material and know what it's about. It's exciting to work on this. It's going to take me a decade. Right now it's my night job. I do about a chapter a year. I look at the project as if it were a mountain. I'm not going to climb many more mountains, but this is a mountain worth climbing. It's a project that will keep me interested in the world and keep me working. I think of it as kind of a companion as I age.

I'm working on a book now about the lyrics of composer Yip Harburg. "Seize the day" is what he says in all of his lyrics. Two of his brothers died at a very early age. He's always reminding you to get your jug of wine while you still have your senses. Don't postpone life. He does it in such a charming way. He's says in three lines in lyrics he wrote for the musical *Bloomer Girl* what I've gone on about for an hour now:

> I gotta song,
> Gotta railroad and a woman and a singer song,
> Gotta sing 'em when you're living 'cause you're dead so long.

I'm insulted by the notion of not being here because I'm just learning to turn a sentence. I feel I'm just getting good at what I do. I have projects that I want to finish. I want to see my son get married, and I'd like to make a few things righter than they are. I hope I'll be given that privilege. I know I'm in control of my decisions, but it's really a crap shoot. Living my life in a sacramental way doesn't mean belonging to any particular church. It's not just giving lip service to the reverence for life but really feeling it, like the way I feel music when I'm dancing, or the way I feel when I catch a fish.

I see life as an endlessly interesting and complicated struggle. Sometimes I see something that is so beautiful that I'll get very emotional about it, because I know I won't always be able to see it. It will go away or I will go away. It depresses you, but at the same time it emboldens you to appreciate what you have.

One of my dearest friends died this year. It was a heart-rending thing. Yet his death was a blessing, I just couldn't see it at the time. He was a wonderful, inspiring, stoic individual. I hope I can be as brave and dignified and stoic and accepting. If I'm allowed to live myself out, I hope that I would be like him. It's one of the paradoxes of life, that suffering brings a kind of understanding of life. I struggle with this thought every day. It does something to me to make me be in life in a better way. Part of living life is really taking it in. I'm in the business of taking life in; I'm a professional "taker-inner" of life. Half of my colleagues from college are already retired. Retired? God might retire me one day, but until that time I'm going to go for it. As long as I'm functioning and wanting to be in the world, as long as I'm alive and expressing the spirit, that's the adventure and the mission. Like the title of your book, *The Ageless Spirit*. What does "spirit" mean? "Spirit" means breath, and that means not just taking it in but expelling it, letting it out, expressing yourself. That's what I want to continue to do.

About the Editor

> ⇥   ⇥   ⇥   ⇥   ⇥   ⇥   ⇥   ⇥   ⇥

Connie Goldman is an award-winning independent public radio producer, author, and public speaker, formerly on the staff of National Public Radio. She is the author of four books, including The Gifts of Caregiving (Fairview Press, 2002), and is the recipient of the 2001 Senior Award from the American Society on Aging. She lives near the Twin Cities of Minneapolis and St. Paul, Minnesota.